SUCCESSFUL ORAL AND WRITTEN PRESENTATIONS

Successful Oral and Written Presentations

Lassor A. Blumenthal

A PERIGEE BOOK

Perigee Books
are published by
The Putnam Publishing Group
200 Madison Avenue
New York, NY 10016

Library of Congress Cataloging-in-Publication Data

Blumenthal, Lassor A.
    Successful oral and written presentations.

    (The Practical handbook series)
    1. Communication in management.   2. Oral
communication.   3. Business writing.   I. Title.
HF5718.B57   1987   658.4′5   87-2272
ISBN 0-399-51330-2

Printed in the United States of America
        2   3   4   5   6   7   8   9   10

Typeset by Fisher Composition, Inc.

TO MY FAMILY

Contents

1. How to Begin

WHAT A GOOD PRESENTATION CAN MEAN TO YOU

Preparing and delivering a good presentation benefits you in two ways: you do good for others, and for yourself. You do good for others because you help them be wiser: you tell them things they did not know. And you do good for yourself because your audience is grateful to you for enlightening them.

In this book, you'll learn how to achieve that double benefit by making effective written and spoken presentations. Let's begin with some suggestions for overcoming what is often the biggest obstacle to a successful presentation: fear.

HOW TO DEAL WITH YOUR FEARS

If you're like many people, you find that the most difficult part of writing and delivering a presentation is getting started. Fear is the obstacle. Fear of not knowing where to begin. Fear of using the wrong words, or the wrong grammar, or the wrong ideas. And fear that people may laugh at you, or not understand you.

If you've never prepared a presentation before, or if you've never prepared one as important as the one you're about to prepare, then you can relax: you're perfectly justified in feeling afraid.

In a sense, you're in the same situation as a child learning to take its first steps alone. It's a frightening process because there's nothing to hold on to—no parent's hand, no table leg. And of course, if you're a child learning to walk, you inevitably will fall. And you may feel some discomfort and frustration. But you get up and start again. And fall again. And get up again. And of course, eventually, you *will* reach your destination. And the next time you start to walk, you'll fall less frequently. And soon, you won't fall at all.

TAKING STEPS TO A SUCCESSFUL PRESENTATION

This analogy is a good one to remember when dealing with your fears about preparing a presentation. Because the preparation is simply a series of small steps, each step will take you a little closer to your destination, and eventually you'll get there quite successfully.

So, while your worries are justified, you can give even more weight to your expectations: the fact is, you *can* write a fine presentation.

WHAT YOU'LL LEARN FROM THIS BOOK

One of your first steps is figuring out where to start—and there are simple techniques you'll learn in this chapter. Another step is organizing your ideas. We discuss that in chapter 2. Still another step is doing research and organizing it. You'll find that in chapters 3 and 4. Then comes the writing—and you'll get help on that in chapter 5. Chapter 6 will help you make your presentation physically attractive on paper, while chapters 7 through 10 will show you how to be a more effective speaker. Chapter 11 will explain how to get help from professional consultants.

This is not a long book, but it's filled with the essentials you need to reach your goal: preparing and delivering a successful presentation.

YOUR BASIC TOOLS

To start, you'll need the simplest of tools: a pen or pencil, and paper. Be generous with the paper because you're probably going to throw lots of it away. This, in fact, is Blumenthal's First Law of Presentation Preparation: *Paper exists to be thrown away.*

What kind of paper should you have? I frequently work with a college-ruled, spiral-bound notebook. The spiral wire binding makes it easy to write with the book wide open, or with the pages folded under one another. And it also keeps the pages in order.

Some people prefer wide-ruled sheets while others prefer narrow-ruled ones. Some prefer blank paper to lined. Others like loose-leaf notebooks, or journals with stitched or glued-in pages. Still others prefer loose sheets of paper—although this increases the risk of mixed-up page sequences. (You can diminish that problem by getting in the habit of numbering your pages before writing on them.)

You may also find it helpful to have a supply of index cards. They come in four sizes—3″ × 5″, 4″ × 6″, 5″ × 8″ and 6″ × 9″, plain or with ruled lines on one side, and in a variety of colors. Some people prefer to work on index cards, and in the next chapter, we'll describe how they can be quite useful.

Still others, of course, prefer to compose on a word processor. I use one for my presentations, not because it helps me to think more clearly (it doesn't), but because it greatly decreases retyping time for subsequent drafts.

When it comes to your writing implements, use whatever gives you not only satisfaction, but joy. If you like a certain color of ink, or a certain hardness of pencil, by all means, use it. Writing has many kinds of pleasures, not the least of them the satisfaction of using one's favorite tools.

MAKE YOURSELF COMFORTABLE

It will help you think more clearly if you put yourself in a comfortable environment both physically and mentally. So if you possibly can, start working in a quiet place, free from distractions, where you will be able to devote adequate time to the project and will be relaxed but mentally alert. This is especially important at the beginning of a presentation, when you have to do your most creative work.

THINK ABOUT YOUR AUDIENCE

Every presentation involves at least two important people—yourself and the person to whom you're making the presentation. This is true whether you're dashing off a memo, writing a term paper or a letter, or giving a formal report.

Of course, your presentation may involve many more than two people, as when you're circulating a memo to a group, or writing a report for a panel, or delivering a speech to an audience.

We begin with the audience because getting your message across to them successfully is the main reason for making your presentation.

Thinking about the audience first may seem to be going at the job backwards. After all, isn't your main concern to say what *you* want to say—not what your audience may want to hear?

The answer is yes and no. Yes, if you're writing poetry. It's unlikely that a poet would begin a poem by thinking: "What does my audience want to hear about springtime?" And certainly, it's true of other kinds of creative writing, too.

But after you've delivered a presentation, you want people to *do* something or *believe* something.

• If you're delivering a paper on the results of your research, you want the audience to believe that you've done a thorough job, and that you've reached valid conclusions. And, depending on the circumstances, you may also anticipate a reward, such as a high grade, a promotion or a research grant.

• If you're a sales manager explaining a new product to your sales force, you want them leave with a clear understanding of the product, and you also want them to go out and sell it enthusiastically.

• And if you're the chairperson of a task force making a report to the board that appointed you, you want to make sure that they understand and will follow your recommendations.

Just as a compass helps keep you on the most direct route to your destination when you're traveling across uncharted areas, thinking about your audience helps you decide to include in your presentation, and how to organize it so that the audience will be interested in it and understand it.

Here, then, is a list of questions to ask yourself about your audience. I recommend that you write down each question at the top of a page. Then write down your answers. Start each answer with a new paragraph, and number them sequentially. This will help you to see each answer clearly, and later, to shift them around easily if you wish.

Who is my main audience?

The answer may be simple: it may be your boss, a subordinate or a teacher. It may be a group: club members or departmental colleagues. Write down a brief description of this main audience.

Are there other audiences besides my main audience?

Often, others besides your main audience will hear or read your presentation. Their interests may be the same as, or different from, those of your main audience. You'll want to think about what these differences are, and whether your presentation should take them into account.

For example, you may be a marketing manager talking to a group of engineers. However, one or two top executives in the company may also be present, evaluating your potential for a higher position. In that case, you can help yourself by adding some information that will especially interest them.

Or you may be writing a presentation for your boss. But might she pass it on to her boss? Or, if you're making a presentation to your subordinates, might people in other departments also be present?

Being aware of these secondary audiences, and of what you want them to think or do, can strengthen your presentation significantly. So make a list of all the people who might be seeing or hearing your presentation.

What do I want my main audience to do as a result of my presentation?

Virtually every presentation attempts to make the audience think or act in a certain way. Before you begin researching or writing your presentation, it will be useful to list the things you want your main audience to think or do.

Do you want them to carry out a policy you've enunciated? Do you want them to stop doing something they've been doing—or do something they haven't been doing? Do you want them to fund you, or follow you? And do you want them to do more than one thing? Do you perhaps want them to do two or three things?

After you've made out your list, with one item to a paragraph, number them in order of importance. This will be a further guide in helping you decide how to organize your presentation.

What do I want my main audience to think or believe as a result of my presentation?

You may not always want the audience to *do* something as a result of your presentation. But you *will* usually want them to think or believe something. It may be that you want them simply to think that you've made an excellent presentation. But more often, you'll want them to learn something, or change their minds, or perhaps believe more firmly in something they already believe.

List the things you want the audience to think or believe, and number them in order of their importance.

What do I want my main audience to feel as a result of my presentation?

Answering this question often takes some serious thinking, because most of us don't usually focus on emotions when we're making a presentation. We tend to think primarily about the information we're transmitting.

But the feelings of your audience will strongly influence how they react to your presentation, so it will be useful to take those feelings into account in your preliminary planning.

For example, you might be preparing to make a presentation proposing new traffic lights for a dangerous intersection in your neighborhood. You'll be more persuasive if you can make your audience feel both the perils of the current situation and the satisfaction they'll have once the lights are installed.

Or suppose that you're making an award at a sales meeting to the winner of a sales contest in your company. Of course, you'll want your audience to admire the winner's achievements. But you'll also want them to feel good about having such a high achiever in their ranks; further, you'll want them to feel motivated to become winners the next time.

Think about the emotions you want to evoke in your main audience, and write them down.

What are the three main things my audience wants to hear from me?

This is a very useful question to ask, because the answers may help you to emphasize certain points that you'd neglect if you thought only about what *you* felt was important. *You* may want to talk about the high price of apples, but the audience may want to hear about the high price of oranges.

Generally, you can get an audience to hear what you want to tell them about if you show them why it's important to them. So, if your audience wants to hear about the high price of oranges, and you want to talk about the high price of apples, you can get their attention by showing how the high price of oranges is related to the high price of apples.

List three things your audience wants to hear from you. And if there are more than three things, list them all, then number them in order of importance. When you come to outline your presentation, you can use this list to make sure you're covering points your audience wants to hear.

What do I want my secondary audience to do, think and feel?

Answer these questions using the same process as when you thought about what you want your main audience to do.

> NOW, PREPARE A CAREFUL ANSWER FOR
> THE MOST IMPORTANT QUESTION OF ALL:

What are the three most important points I want my main audience to take away with them?

It is usually difficult to gain and keep the attention of an audience, whether the audience is one person reading your presentation, or a group hearing you speak.

Attention spans are short. Distractions are abundant. The audience rarely has enough time to give your ideas the close study they deserve. And if you're not absolutely clear about what you want them to know, they will understand little and remember less.

You can make your presentation much clearer if you write down a list of the most important points you want your audience to keep in mind. If you're writing a short note, you may have only a single point. But if it's a longer presentation, you may have several.

Under the heading "The Points I Want the Audience to Remember," list *all* the major things you want them to keep in mind, using a separate paragraph for each point.

Next, number them in order of importance.

When you've numbered the list, review it once again to see if any items are really part of the other items, and should be included as subordinate ideas. For example, imagine that you've been asked to do some research and recommend which of two brands of computers your organization should buy. When you're ready to write your recommendations, you sit down and think: what are the most important points I want the audience to remember?

Probably one thought that will occur to you is the name of the computer you're recommending. So, you write that down:

1. I recommend buying the Whippet Model T computer.

Then, you'll probably come up with reasons for your recommendation:

2. People in other organizations like ours recommend it.
3. It's economical.
4. It's compatible with IBM, the industry standard.
5. We can get a very good price from the local dealer.
6. It's a very rugged machine.
7. The manufacturer has been in business a long time and will probably be around for a long time to come.
8. It's an easy machine to service if it breaks down.
9. *Consumer Reports* magazine rates it number one.

As you study your list, it becomes evident that some items are duplicates, or at least closely related. For example, items 3 and 5 are both about price. Items 2 and 9 both refer to evaluations by other people. You can combine these pairs, and come up with a second list:

1. I recommend buying the Whippet Model T computer.
2. It's highly recommended by other organizations like ours, and *Consumer Reports* rates it number one.
3. The price is low, and we can get a very good deal from the local dealer.
4. It's compatible with IBM, the industry standard.
5. It's a very rugged machine.

6. The manufacturer has been in business a long time and will probably be around for a long time to come.
7. It's an easy machine to service if it breaks down.

Next, you'll put the items in order of their importance. And here is where you'll find it useful to think about your audience. For example, if you're preparing the report for your boss, who is very concerned about reliability, you'll probably lead off with the items that emphasize reliability:

1. I recommend buying the Whippet Model T computer.
2. It's highly recommended by other organizations like ours, and *Consumer Reports* rates it number one.
3. It's a very rugged machine.
4. The manufacturer has been in business a long time and will probably be around for a long time to come.
5. It's compatible with IBM, the industry standard.
6. The price is low, and we can get a very good deal from the local dealer.
7. It's an easy machine to service if it breaks down.

Or, if you're making the presentation for the firm's treasurer, who's very concerned about costs, you might place first the items that refer to cost:

1. I recommend buying the Whippet Model T computer.
2. The price is low, and we can get a very good deal from the local dealer.
3. It's an easy machine to service if it breaks down.
4. It's a very rugged machine.
5. The manufacturer has been in business a long time and will probably be around for a long time to come.
6. It's highly recommended by other organizations like ours, and *Consumer Reports* rates it number one.
7. It's compatible with IBM, the industry standard.

After looking over your list, you may want to revise it still further. For example, you might feel that item 1, your recommendation to buy the Whippet, should come at the end rather than the beginning. Here again, think about your audience. What will impress them most? Organize your report accordingly.

When should you make the list?

If you know pretty well what information you're going to include in your presentation, you may be able to make this list when you sit down to write the presentation.

On the other hand, if you're going to have to do some research before you know what's important, you may not be able to make the list until after you've done the research. Even so, you may find it useful to make the list out at the beginning of your work. It may serve as a help in indicating what kind of research you should undertake in order to prepare a presentation that will be most persuasive.

Now that you've made a start on deciding what to say, you're ready for the next step—making an outline. Chapter 2 tells you how.

2. Making an Outline of Your Presentation

There are many ways to develop an outline, and there is no one right way. You might want to review all of the techniques described here, and then select the one that seems best for your situation.

We can begin by dividing outline construction into two broad categories: outlines based on your first thoughts; and outlines based on research. This chapter will discuss outlines based on your first thoughts—that is, when you have a rough idea of what you want to say. Chapter 3 discusses how to make outlines based on research.

MAKING AN OUTLINE BASED ON FIRST THOUGHTS

Once you've gone through the steps described in chapter 1, you'll have an idea of the kinds of information that will be most appropriate to your presentation. You'll have a clearer idea of the points that you want to make, and of the points that your main and your secondary audiences want to know about.

For your next step, it will be helpful to make an outline that briefly lists the main points you plan to make in your presentation. For example, as I begin to write this chapter about how to prepare an outline, I have an idea of what I want to discuss. One way of writing the chapter is to first make a rough outline, listing the topics I ought to cover. Here are the items that come instantly into my head:

Chapter Two: Outlining
1. What an outline is
2. Expect to change the outline
3. How to organize the outline
   a. Important to write down *all* your ideas

That's as far as I can think it through. Now, I sit back and relax. Then, looking at what I've written, I see that I want to explain *why* I started with the headline, "Chapter Two: Outlining." I decide that such an explanation should come after item 3a. So, I add a new item:

3. How to organize the outline
   a. Important to write down all your ideas
   b. Importance of headline

Now, it occurs to me, I ought to say something about why it's useful to put a number or letter at the beginning of each entry. So, I add that to my outline, also under item 3:

3. How to organize the outline
   a. Important to write down all your ideas
   b. Importance of headline
   c. Use of numbers and letters for clarity

Then I remember one of the basic rules of good presentations: to get the audience's attention at the beginning, explain that what you're going to say is important to them, or how it will benefit them. So, I add that to item 1:

1. What an outline is
   a. Why it's important

Then I recall that in chapter 1 I dealt with the emotional barriers to writing a presentation. And that reminds me that sometimes I feel anxiety about writing an outline. And if *I* feel it, you may also feel it. So, I decide to discuss that near the front of the chapter, and I add it to the outline:

1. What an outline is
   a. Why it's important
2. Dealing with anxiety

Having made this the second item in my outline, I now have to change the remaining numbers. Now, my outline looks like this:

1. What an outline is
   a. Why it's important
2. Dealing with anxiety
3. Expect to change the outline
4. How to organize the outline
   a. Important to write down all your ideas
   b. Importance of headline
   c. Use of numbers and letters for clarity

As I look at this outline, it strikes me that the chapter seems to end rather abruptly. Perhaps I need to add another entry to item 4, or add a concluding item 5. I decide to make up my mind later, after I've written more, and have a clearer idea of what needs to be added.

Now, having just written the paragraph above, one of my favorite quotations pops into my head about anxiety—item 2. (The quotation, from an ancient Chinese book, is: "The heart thinks constantly. This cannot be changed. But the movement of the heart—that is, a man's thoughts—should restrict itself to the immediate situation. All thinking that goes beyond this only makes the heart sore.") I know I may forget to include it in the chapter unless I write it down. So I add to item 2:

  2. Dealing with anxiety
    a. Take it one step at a time—"The heart thinks constantly."

Now I'm ready to continue writing the chapter. (Incidentally, you'll find an alternative approach to outlining in chapter 4, page 36, in the section "Categorize According to Your Materials.")

WHY AN OUTLINE IS IMPORTANT

An outline is important for two reasons:
• If you're not sure of what you want to say, it will help you to decide.
• It will help you to organize your ideas—both to put the most important points first, and to help you to put your related ideas together. In effect, an outline is like a series of stepping stones across a wide stream. The stream represents all the things you *might* put into your presentation. The stepping stones are the important points that you *should* put into your presentation to get from the beginning to the end.

It's true that an outline isn't always helpful. If you're making a very short presentation, or if you've made similar presentations, you may already have a good idea of what you're going to say. You may also prefer simply to think and write your way through your presentation a step at a time. In fact, the more often you write, the easier this will become. But until it becomes easy, making an outline is generally a good idea.

DEALING WITH ANXIETY

As you begin to think about writing your outline, you may sense that you're caught in a dilemma. On the one hand, you may feel that you can't write an outline until after you've done your research. On the other hand, you may not be sure about what kind of research to do until you've made an outline that will direct your research. How can you get out of this difficulty?

As a general rule, you get out of it as we get out of so many traps in life—by taking command. That is, you make a decision to prepare the best outline you can *under the circumstances*. You may have to modify or even throw out the outline and start again when you've progressed further on the presentation. But if you take charge in the beginning, the rest of the process will be much easier.

EXPECT TO CHANGE THE OUTLINE

You may worry about your ability to put together a second outline after you've spent so much time and energy writing the first one. Won't it mean that you've wasted all the effort you put into the first outline?

Not at all! Your first outline is simply a guess about what your final presentation should contain. If you decide to revise your outline later, it will be because your second thoughts are better than your first thoughts. So, discarding your first outline and starting on a new one is not a sign of failure, but a sign of progress. You are moving in the direction you want to go—getting closer to a successful presentation with each succeeding revision. (And remember: that's why in chapter 1 I recommend that you have lots of paper—so that you can throw it away freely when it's no longer useful.)

As I write these words, I notice that I still haven't put in the thought I had entered in the outline as part of item 2:

> a. Take it one step at a time—"The heart thinks constantly."

Thinking about it now, I realize that it doesn't really fit. And so I decide to leave it out. This, of course, is exactly the point I've been making: an outline should be a help to you, not a straitjacket. (Incidentally, if you decide to reject an idea that was in your outline, put it aside, but don't throw it away. You may want to use it later.)

And now, as you read on, you'll see that the rest of this chapter doesn't exactly follow the outline I've so carefully described in the preceding paragraphs. That's because as I began writing, I thought of new points to include. The outline is there, but changed, and, I think, improved.

WAYS TO MAKE OUTLINING EASIER

Here are some suggestions to make the outlining go more easily.

1. Leave your mind alone. It has been observed that our minds have two marvelous abilities: One is the capacity to create; the other, the capacity to criticize. What prevents many of us from creating is that we allow our critical capacity to destroy what we're creating *before* we've created it. An idea pops into our heads, and before we can get it down on paper, we begin to worry about its flaws and deficiencies. Finally, we discard it, and we feel empty and defeated, because we've let our mind-as-critic overwhelm our mind-as-creator.

How do you overcome this problem? It's essentially a matter of willpower. You have to decide that for a certain period you will only create—you will not criticize. You can define that period in any way you want. For example, you might say: "For the next ten minutes (or the next hour, or the next day) I'll write down any ideas that come to me about the outline. I will totally refrain from criticizing them: All the ideas that come to me will be equally acceptable."

Or instead of giving yourself a time limit, you might give yourself a topic limit: "I'm going to think of ten things that might go into my outline. And until I get ten, I will totally refrain from criticizing them; all will be equally acceptable."

This is essentially the same process as that used in brainstorming sessions. A group of people facing a problem freely suggest every solution they can think of, regardless of how silly it seems, and no one offers any criticism. Later, when the brainstorming is finished, the critical process starts and the group selects the best ideas.

2. Write down every idea that comes to you. Our minds are like a vast ocean in which infinite numbers of fascinating creatures—vague ideas, snatches of thought—float quietly into and out of sight. If we capture them, they may become valuable additions to our presentation.

3. Don't worry about the sequence. If you're not sure of where a point should go in your outline, don't worry about it. You can move it into its proper position later. At the beginning, just write down each idea as it comes to you.

So, when you're writing your outline, if vague thoughts come to you, don't push them away, thinking that you'll come back to them later: You may forget them. Instead, stop and make a brief note, and then continue with what you were writing. Then return to the note when you're ready, and develop it more fully.

4. Write a title or a headline. When you're struggling to put ideas on paper, your mind tends to wander, and it's often difficult to remember just what you were supposed to be thinking about. This is especially true if you're uncertain about what you want to say. One way to overcome the problem is to put a title or headline at the top of the page. It serves as a beacon, reminding you to come back to where you belong.

5. Talk to yourself. If you find your mind wandering as you try to create your outline, you may find it helpful to talk your way into the outline. This can be especially useful if you've been trying unsuccessfully to come up with some ideas for your presentation, and you feel your mind is tied up in a knot. Pause for a couple of minutes to relax—get a drink of water, or do something physical for a change of pace.

Then, say out loud: "What I really want to say is . . ." Keep talking—and start writing, as if you were dictating to yourself. This combination of speaking and writing may get you off to a flying start.

6. Use your chapter 1 material. Some of the lists that you made in chapter 1 can be very useful for preparing your outline. One was a list of the three most important points you want your audience to keep in mind. Look at that list now. *It may, in fact, turn out to be the basis for your outline.*

If you feel that this *is* a good beginning, you should also look at the list you made in response to the question "What are the three main things my audience wants to hear from me?" As a general rule, try to include those points in your outline. If they're the same points that you want to tell your audience, then your job is easy. If they're not the same, think about how you can integrate them in a logical flow.

For example, suppose you want to make a fund-raising proposal to the governing board of a charity organization to which you belong. In answer to the question "What are the three main things my audience wants to hear from me?" you've written:

1. How much money can we expect to raise?
2. How many people will have to be involved?
3. Who'll be in charge of organizing it?

And, in answer to the question "What are the three most important points I want my audience to take away with them?" you've written:

1. This is a great idea.
2. We should get started on it now.
3. I'd like to cochair with Bob Dole.

Writing these lists in adjacent columns, rather than one group above the other, makes it easier to draw lines showing how you want to integrate the items.

1. How much money can we raise?	1. This is a great idea.
2. How many people will be involved?	2. We should get started on it now.

3. Who'll be in charge of organizing it?	3. I'd like to cochair with Bob Dole.

Let's say that, to stimulate their interest, you decide to lead with "This is a great idea." You circle that sentence and draw a line from it to the top of the left column.

You decide that "We should get started on it now" is probably a good way to end your proposal. So, you circle that sentence and draw a line from it to the bottom of the left column.

And finally, you decide that "I'd like to cochair with Bob Dole" belongs right after "Who'll be in charge of organizing it?"

Now your list looks like this:

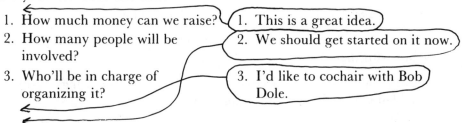

Next, rewrite your outline so that you can see the ideas in their new order:

Fund-Raising Proposal
1. This is a great idea
2. How much money we can raise
3. How many people will be involved
4. Who'll be in charge of organizing it
5. I'd like to cochair with Bob Dole
6. We should get started on it now

As you look at your outline, you may want to change it. For example, you say that this is a great idea, but you don't say why it's a great idea. Further, you don't say what the idea is; you'll certainly want to describe it near the beginning. And you may be able to eliminate point 4, "Who'll be in charge of organizing it," because it's covered by point 5. So, your next version of the outline looks like this.

Fund-Raising Proposal
1. This is a great idea
2. What the idea is
3. Why it's a great idea
4. How much money we can raise
5. How many people will be involved
6. I'd like to cochair with Bob Dole
7. We should get started on it now

When you're satisfied that this pretty much covers your main points, you're ready to start writing your presentation. In chapter 5, we'll actually do it.

GOOD BEGINNINGS

A good presentation has a logical beginning, middle and end. If you've put together an outline as the previous section described, you probably already have established that logical flow.

But it's a good idea to take one more step to make sure you're on the right track; that is, to think about your beginning and your ending.

First, consider your beginning. One excellent way to decide what it should be is to ask yourself: "What background does my audience need in order to understand my presentation?"

If they're familiar with the subject, they'll need little or no background—perhaps just one or two sentences to let them know what the presentation is about. Here are some typical ways to begin:

Jump right in: "This memo is about XYZ," or "This memo deals with XYZ."

Explain its importance: "XYZ is a subject of wide concern, and this paper deals with that issue."

Update: "Last week we discussed XYZ, and this memo brings us up to date on what's been done about it since then."

Cheer it on: "XYZ is a project that many of us believe will fulfill a valuable function. In this memo, I'll explain what it is and why we should put it into effect."

If they're not familiar with the subject, begin by giving as much background as they need in order to follow the rest of your presentation. The four categories in the previous section can serve you here, as well. That is:

Jump right in: "This memo is about XYZ. It's an important subject because . . ." (Now supply the reason why it's important to your audience.)

Explain its importance: "XYZ is a subject of wide concern, and this paper deals with that issue. A little background will be helpful." (Now continue with the background.)

Update: "Last week we discussed XYZ, and this memo brings us up to date on what's been done about it since then. For those of you who missed our discussion, here's a summary." (Continue with the summary, then give the update.)

Cheer it on: "XYZ is a project that many of us believe will fulfill a valuable function. In this memo, I'll explain what it is and why we should put it into effect." (This version is the same as the version for an audience that's familiar with your subject: in both cases, you explain the background.)

HOW TO END

After you've decided on your beginning, think about your presentation's ending. Look at your outline and select the most important point—the one you want your audience to remember above all others. Generally, this is the point to end with, even though you may have mentioned it before.

Often, you'll find that the idea you began with will serve quite nicely for an ending. You may also want to couple that beginning idea with a call to action or a recommendation for the audience to think about what you've said.

Here are the four beginnings from above, each followed by two endings—one a call to action, the other a recommendation for further thought.

1. *"Jump right in" beginning:* "This memo is about XYZ. It's an important subject because . . ." (Now supply the reasons why it's important to your audience.)

   "Call to action" ending: "As I said at the beginning, XYZ is an important subject. For the reasons explained in this memo, I recommend that we meet next week to discuss it further."

   "Further thought" ending: "For all these reasons, it's important that we learn from XYZ, and think about its implications for our future."

2. *"Explain its importance" beginning:* "XYZ is a subject of wide concern, and this paper deals with that issue. A little background will be helpful." (Now continue with the background.)

   "Call to action" ending: "Because of the wide concern with this issue, we should take the following steps." (Now outline the steps to be taken.)

   "Further thought" ending: "Thus there are many reasons why this issue is of widespread concern. Research may help to provide effective solutions in the future."

3. *"Update" beginning:* "Last week we discussed XYZ, and this memo brings us up to date on what's been done about it since then. For those of you who missed our discussion, here's a summary." (Continue with the summary, then give the update.)

   "Call to action" ending: "Given this update, I think it makes sense to do ABC."

   "Further thought" ending: "No action is needed at this point, but I'll plan on sending another memo on this subject next week to keep you on top of it."

4. *"Cheer it on" beginning:* "XYZ is a project that many of us believe will fulfill a valuable function. In this memo, I'll explain what it is and why we should put it into effect."

   "Call to action" ending: "You can see why this is so important. Now let's act on it."

   "Further thought" ending: "In view of the subject's importance, I'm asking each of you to think about how you might play a role in making it happen. We'll talk about it at our next meeting."

3. How to Research

A WORD ABOUT WORRY

As is true for virtually every aspect of a good presentation, your mental and emotional attitudes will influence the efficiency and the thoroughness of your research.

For example, you may find it difficult to write presentations because you fear your research will be inadequate, and that you'll be criticized for your ignorance. Or you may worry that between the time you finish researching and the time you make your presentation, new developments will make your work obsolete.

To reduce your anxiety, keep in mind that your audience will probably not know as much about the subject as you do, simply because they will not have done the research you've done. Your research will help turn you into more of an authority, a person to whom others look for information.

Obviously, there's another side to the coin: there may be people in your audience who know as much as, or more than, you, and who disagree with you. But that, of course, is a good way to learn and to grow.

This chapter may not eliminate your worries about research, but it will give you some useful suggestions that will help you win praise for the thoroughness of your presentation.

DEFINE YOUR RESEARCH QUESTIONS

Regardless of how little or how much research your presentation will require, the first thing to do is to write down a list of the questions or the issues for which you want answers. The list will enable you to confine your research to just those areas you're interested in. Be as specific as you can.

Here, for example, are four increasingly specific entries:

1. Washing machines
2. The history of washing machines
3. The history of washing machines from 1900 to 1930
4. The history of washing machines from 1900 to 1930 in France

If you're writing a presentation about washing machines in general, entry 1 would be adequate for your needs, and you might go directly to a general encyclopedia for your research.

The information for entry 2 might also be found in a general encyclopedia, but you might have to also look in an encyclopedia of technology or the social sciences.

Entries 3 and 4 are increasingly detailed; the simple act of writing them down will give you some thoughts about more specialized sources where you might find the necessary information.

That's why writing down your research questions in as much detail as you can will often help you to save time by suggesting the most likely sources.

PEOPLE AS RESOURCES

Your research will probably be based on interviews with people or on written materials. First, let's examine ways to make your research with people more effective.

Choose a satisfactory paper format

In advance of your interview, decide on the paper format that will be most convenient for recording your notes. Here are some options to consider:

Wire-bound notebooks: Spiral wire-bound books come in several sizes, from 3″ × 5″ up to 8½″ × 11″. Smaller sizes fit conveniently in one hand, leaving the other hand free for writing—useful if you're taking notes standing up.

All sizes are available with the wire binding along the side or the top. I like the side-bound style because it's easier for me to write on both sides of the sheet. But this is a matter of personal preference, and you should select whatever style pleases you.

Wire-bounds have various refinements. The lines on the page are available in wide-ruled and narrow- (or college-) ruled. The narrow-ruled lines let you squeeze more lines on the page, and as long as you can write small and legibly, they're fine. Some wire-bounds have three holes so that the whole notebook, or individual sheets, can be filed in loose-leaf notebooks. Some have page perforations parallel to the binding to make sheet removal easier. Some have dividers, and some dividers have tabs.

Loose-leaf binders: The three-ring format is standard. Its advantage is that you can easily add and remove pages. Its disadvantages are that the binding makes it bulkier than the wire-bound format, and that you can't fold the front cover against the back, which you can do with the wire-bounds, and which is often convenient when note-taking.

Memo books are loose-leaf binders in smaller sizes, ranging from 3″ × 5″ to about 4″ × 7″. They usually have six rings.

Loose leaf pages come narrow- and wide-ruled, and dividers are available, with or without tabs.

Write your questions in advance

If you have more than one or two questions to ask your interviewee, write them out before the interview so that you'll be sure to get answers to all of them.

Leave space for the answers

Plan in advance about where you're going to write your answers to the questions you ask. For example, if you know that the answers will be relatively brief, write the questions one after the other on a sheet of paper, leaving enough space after each question to fit in the answers.

If the answers are likely to be long, write each question at the top of a fresh sheet of paper, and leave the rest of the page for the response. This arrangement also gives you plenty of room to add material if, later in the interview, the interviewee refers to an earlier question.

If you're going to ask more than one person the same questions, consider preparing a fresh copy of your questions for each interview, so that you can write each person's answers on a separate page, and then collate them later.

Consider using index cards

You may find it more convenient to write each question at the top of an index card, and to write the interviewee's answers below. Refer to page 32 for more information on index cards.

Decide on the type of interview

There are, broadly speaking, two types of interviews: structured and unstructured. In a structured interview, you ask a very specific question, record the answer, and go on to the next specific question. Generally, you'll have a structured interview when you're looking for specific facts. For example, the questions and answers might go like this:

> Q: How many pieces did we make last year?
> A: About five thousand.
> Q: How does that compare with the year before?
> A: It's about a ten percent increase.
> Q: What about next year's production?
> A: It'll be about ten percent higher again.

In an unstructured interview, you encourage the interviewee to speak at length about the subject. Unstructured interviews are good for exploring opinions and attitudes. An unstructured interview might go like this:

> Q: How many pieces did we make last year?
> A: About five thousand.
> Q: Were you surprised with that number?
> A: Yes, frankly, I was.
> Q: Why was that?

A: Well, with the strike and all, plus the overseas competition, I thought we'd be down considerably.

Q: Why didn't the strike and the foreign competition affect production?

Here, the interviewer is probing for information by asking the interviewee for opinions and explanations. The interviewer wrote out the first question; the rest were based on the interviewee's replies. It generally takes a bit of experience to conduct an unstructured interview, but it's worth practicing because it frequently turns up information that can be useful in your presentation.

Setting up appointments

If you need brief answers to only one or two questions, you may be able to get them with just an informal telephone call, or a casual in-person visit. But if the interviews will take longer than that, it's a good idea to set up an appointment for a mutually convenient time. This will help to insure that you'll have adequate time to get the information you want.

If you think the interviewee will have to do some research or some thinking to come up with answers, it can be helpful to provide him or her in advance with a written list of your questions. This will let you make the best use of your time, and may help you to get fuller answers than if the interviewee had to answer you without preparation.

Should you use a tape recorder?

Tape-recording an interview has both advantages and drawbacks. The main advantage is that you'll accurately capture your interviewee's remarks. This helps to eliminate misquotes or misinterpretations, particularly if you're not completely familiar with what the interviewee is talking about.

A major disadvantage is that many people tend to censor themselves in front of a tape recorder. So taping may be an obstacle if you're looking for maximum honesty or maximum spontaneity.

Another disadvantage is that recording is not a fool-proof procedure. The tape may end without your realizing it before the end of the interview; the machine may break down; or the interviewee may not speak clearly or loudly enough. So when I tape-record interviews, I also take copious notes. I generally find them adequate for my needs, but the tapes will occasionally provide additional useful information that I neglected to write down.

If you plan on taping an interview, courtesy dictates that you ask the interviewee's permission first. As you're setting up the machine, you can simply ask, "Do you mind if I tape the interview?" Or, if you're less self-confident, you can explain: "I'd like to be sure that I'm getting an accurate record of your answers. Do you mind if I tape-record them?" If the interviewee objects, then put away the machine.

What's the best tape recorder for interviews? There are so many choices, and so many new ones are regularly being introduced, that it's largely a matter of deciding what's best for your needs and for your budget. Virtually all portable machines will give you good, if not high, fidelity.

Two points to think about are the size of the audio cassette and the length of the recording. Standard audio cassettes can play as long as forty-five minutes on a side, or ninety minutes on both sides. However, ninety-minute cassettes use a very thin tape which may get caught in the winding mechanism, so most manufacturers recommend using tapes with a maximum playing time of sixty minutes, or thirty minutes on a side.

Increasingly popular are microcassettes, which are about one-fourth the size of standard cassettes, and which play on machines about the size of a king-size pack of cigarettes. The sound quality is not as high as on the standard cassettes, but their lightness and compactness are attractive.

If your interviews are likely to last longer than the length of one side of the tape, consider buying a machine that automatically reverses itself at the end and continues recording on the other side, or a machine that has a switch that allows the tape to move at half the normal speed, thus doubling the recording time. Such machines allow you to record for as long as two hours on one sixty-minute cassette.

Taking Notes: Five rules and one suggestion

The first rule of note-taking is to be sure that you have something to take notes with. Running out of ink or pencil lead or paper in the middle of the interview— or forgetting to bring them with you—is an unnecessary embarrassment.

The second rule of note-taking is to be sure that you'll understand your notes after the interview. This means that you should write clearly enough so that you can read what you've written.

Equally important, you should have the confidence to interrupt if your interviewee is speaking too fast or is not clear. Novice interviewers often hesitate to do this, fearing they'll be thought rude, or that they'll interrupt the creative flow of ideas. So they trust to fate, and hope they'll be able to remember the details after the interview.

The fear is groundless. If you're falling behind, you can politely call a halt: "Excuse me, but I'm falling behind in my notes. Will you give me a second to catch up?" Interviewees are almost invariably happy to give you the extra time you need: after all, you're flattering them by paying attention to their every word.

The third rule of note-taking (and this applies to both interviews and research on written materials) is to write down your sources. At the very least, make certain that at the beginning of each interview, your notes identify the person you're speaking to. Be certain that you've spelled the person's name and affiliation correctly.

If you're interviewing two or more people simultaneously, identify each speaker by writing his/her initials before each comment. When you write your presentation, knowing who said what can be quite helpful.

The fourth rule is to write on one side of the sheet. That will make it easier for you to organize your ideas when you're getting ready to write. This is particularly true if you have a lot of notes, and you want to spread them out, say, on the floor, so that you can see what you've written. (This is discussed in some detail in "Organizing Your Research," chapter 4.) Admittedly, writing on one side wastes paper, but remember that one of the basic rules of a good presentation is that paper was made to be wasted.

The fifth rule is to use abbreviations, because they'll help you take notes faster and more accurately. Shorthand, of course, is ideal. Lacking that, make up symbols for common words, such as *w* for *with*, + for *and*, / for *the*, etc.

A suggestion: After an interview, you may want to insure that the interviewee won't object if you quote his or her statements. In this case, send the person a typed copy of your notes for confirmation. It's a good idea to put a deadline on any corrections the person wants to make. A typical short note might go like this:

Dear Sally,

Thanks for your help the other day. I'm enclosing a copy of the quotes I may use. If I don't hear from you by June 10, I'll assume everything is okay. Thanks again,

Joan

RESEARCH ON WRITTEN MATERIALS

If your presentation can benefit from research on written materials, you can usually draw on a large number of resources. Let's look at some useful ones.

Local files in your office or organization are a good place to begin. If your presentation continues work that you or others have previously written about, those presentations may be a source of useful information. If you're not sure what has been done previously, ask your colleagues.

The public library is an invaluable source of research material, and the right place to begin is with the librarian, who will steer you in the right direction.

Specialized libraries exist in many locations. In New York City, for example, there are more than a dozen, ranging from the Mercantile Library Association to the French Institute–Alliance Française to the New York Law Institute to the Sex Information and Education Council-Resource Center and Library. Look in the yellow pages of your local telephone book, under such headings as "Libraries—Circulating & Rental" and "Libraries—Institutional."

Trade and professional associations often maintain archives relating to their specialties. Again, the yellow pages is a good place to start. Look under such headings as Associations, Business and Trade Organizations, Clubs, Fraternal Organizations, Political Organizations, Social Service Organizations, and Veterans and Military Organizations. Your public library will probably have directories of state, national and international associations.

Periodicals such as magazines, trade and professional journals, newsletters and newspapers can all provide valuable information. To find out which issue of which periodical has the information you want, you can look through one of the indexes to periodicals in the library. Among the most widely consulted are:

Readers' Guide—indexes a large number of periodicals
Book Review Digest—offers digests of book reviews from various journals
Chemical Abstracts—summarizes articles from many journals
New York Times Index—lists all articles in that newspaper

Again, your librarian can direct you to the sources that will be most valuable for your needs.

Reference works can give you information about virtually any subject. A good place to start is the *Guide to Reference Books*, edited by Eugene T. Sheehy, which tells what references are available on virtually every subject under the sun. Here are some of the most popular types of reference works.

Encyclopedias—There are both general encyclopedias like *The New Encyclopedia Britannica*, and a multitude of specialized works, such as *The International Encyclopedia of the Social Sciences*.

Atlases and gazetteers—There are many kinds, some devoted to political affairs, some to history, some to economics, and so on.

Biographical Dictionaries—Two widely used references are the *Dictionary of American Biography* and the *Dictionary of National Biography*, which cover, respectively, deceased Americans and Britons. For contemporary notables, there are such volumes as *Who's Who, Current Biographies* and a variety of books which focus on a single field, such as music, industry or religion.

Chronologies—This category covers books of historical facts. Helpful volumes on America include: Johnson's *Oxford Companion to American History* and Scribner's *Dictionary of American History*. Numerical facts appear in the *Historical Statistics of the United States* and *Statistical Abstract of the United States*.

Dictionaries—The types of dictionaries are almost beyond belief to those familiar with them. To mention just a few, there are language and literature dictionaries, dictionaries of quotations, concordances of the Bible and of famous authors, dictionaries of classical terms, dictionaries of art and architecture and music, and of science and technology.

We can repeat here what we've already said: your local librarian can be extremely helpful in helping you do your research successfully.

RECORDING YOUR WRITTEN RESEARCH

In order to make it easier to organize your material after you've finished researching, make a practice of recording each piece of information on a separate index card, 3″ × 5″ or larger. How much should you record on a card? Think of each piece of information as a single brick that you'll be using someplace in the structure of your presentation. So the information you record should be complete; you should be able to understand it without having to depend on another piece of information on a separate card. (If another card carries more information on the same subject, then make a note on the first card that will enable you to find the second card quickly if you need it.)

The headline: Write a headline at the top of the front of every card. It should tell you at a glance the subject of the material on the card. Write or print it in large letters, on a line by itself, so that it stands out clearly.

Experience will teach you what kind of headline will best serve your needs. It might be a broad topic heading: *Desserts*. Or, you may want more detail: *Desserts, Chocolate*. Or even more detail: *Chocolate Desserts, Sales of*. Or the headlines may be the name of a person or an institution—or anything else that will let you identify the subject matter of the card quickly.

If you think that you may want to change the headline later, write it in pencil, so that you can erase it.

Source of the information

Make a practice of writing down on each card all the information you'll need to find your source again quickly. You may or may not need to include this information in your presentation in a footnote or a bibliography, but it's always comforting to know that you can back up your research with the exact source. Here are some widely accepted formats for footnotes, which you can adapt to your needs.

For a magazine article, cite the author, the name of the article in quotes, the name of the periodical in italics, the volume number, the date, and the pages:

> Howard Jesperson, "My Life in the Wilderness," *Wilderness Frontiers* 23 (June 1987): 23–25.

(In a typed manuscript, underlining the name of the magazine is equivalent to putting it in italics.)

For a book, list the most important information first, whether it's the author, the name of the book, or the editor. Follow this with the publisher, the city where the book was published, and the publication date.

> Jane Rider, *Politics and Princes*, Inkman Publishers, New York, 1980.
> *Politics and Princes*, Jane Rider, Inkman Publishers, New York, 1980.
> Jane Rider, ed., *Politics and Princes*, Inkman Publishers, New York, 1980.

Footnotes referring to books frequently leave out the page number reference, but it's a good idea for you to include it in your own notes to yourself, in case you want to re-examine the source.

This section has dealt mainly with your own notes to yourself. But, if you're interested in knowing a great deal more about the correct use of footnotes, and preparing materials for the printer, refer to a style manual; one used widely is the *Manual of Style*, published by the University of Chicago Press.

4. Organizing Your Research

Experienced researchers set up filing systems *before* they begin their investigations. The reason, of course, is that a good filing system lets you find what you need quickly. As a result, you can easily tell what you have in hand, and equally important, what you don't have, but need to get.

Most of us, however, are not experienced researchers. We tend to gather our material and then try to put it into some sort of order so that we can develop it into a logical presentation. For example, you may have gathered several kinds of material: notes on index cards; other notes that you've made in a notebook; magazine articles; newspaper clippings; photocopies of book pages; illustrations and charts, etc. How do you pull all this together so that the right information goes in precisely the right spot? There are many ways to go about it, and in this chapter, we'll consider some of the most common ones.

CATEGORIZE ACCORDING TO YOUR OUTLINE

Let's assume that you've been assembling material. You think you have enough to make a good presentation, but you're not certain. And you're worried that you may have left some gaps that should be filled in. What should you do?

If you followed the recommendations in chapter 2, you've outlined the major points in your presentation. That outline can now help you to organize your research.

1. Start with file folders

One good way to begin is to obtain several 9″ × 11″, letter-size file folders. Get the kind with a tab projecting above the top, because you'll be writing on it.

2. Mark the file folder tabs

On each tab, write down one of the topics in your outline. If you have to abbreviate, use words that will quickly bring the whole topic to mind, to reduce the possibility of misfiling your material. For example, if your topic is "Benefits of Open Heart Surgery," you might abbreviate it "OHS Benefits."

3. Sort your material into the folders

Now, distribute your research materials into the folders where you think they belong. You may find that some materials don't fit any of your topics. For the time being, put them into another folder marked "Miscellaneous."

Once this job is done, if you have folders with little or no information in them, you'll have a clearer idea of what areas need additional research.

Incidentally, index cards and smaller pieces of paper tend to slide out of file folders lying on a table. You can prevent this annoyance by storing the folders upright in a drawer or box. Wedge them into the upright position so that they can't collapse in the container.

4. Organize each folder

Now, go through each folder and put the research material in a sequence that makes sense to you. Later, when you start writing, you may decide to change the sequence, but this step will give you a very good feeling for the contents of your finished presentation.

5. Unify the sizes for easier handling

The materials in a folder may be different sizes: standard 8½″ × 11″ paper; small brochures; columns of newspaper type. These variations can make it awkward to organize them neatly. You'll find them easier to handle if you fasten them to sheets of 8½″ × 11″ paper with Scotch tape, staples or glue. Index cards can often be treated the same way, although if your research consists mainly of cards, a rubber band will keep them well ordered.

6. Analyze the "Miscellaneous" folder

When you go through the "Miscellaneous" folder, you'll often find that, on second glance, some of the materials belong in folders you've already marked. You may also find that other materials deserve their own folders. So, your presentation will become more detailed and more thorough.

And after you've finished going through the miscellaneous file, you may have material left in it that doesn't fit anyplace in your presentation. Be smart: leave the material there until the presentation is written. You may find that you need it after all, once you start writing.

7. Use a bulletin board

Some people find it helpful to use a large bulletin board for organizing their research. They copy each file folder title on a separate index card, and tack the cards to the bulletin board in horizontal rows. Then they move the cards about until they're in the right sequence.

CATEGORIZE ACCORDING TO YOUR MATERIALS

If you haven't made an outline, your research material can help you to construct one. A basic requirement: give yourself plenty of working space. A large table or the floor can be ideal.

Incidentally, I find this a wonderfully relaxing process because it's almost totally mechanical, involving only minimal use of the brain.

Let's assume that you have a diverse assortment of research material, such as notes on index cards and on pieces of paper; articles; and graphic materials such as photos and charts. Put it all into a pile.

1. Put a topic word or phrase on each piece

Begin by going through the material and writing at the top of the first page of each piece of a one-, two- or three-word description of its main subject. Do it in pencil because you may want to change it later.

2. Lay out the materials

Now, lay each piece down on the surface in front of you. When you come to a piece that has the same heading as one you've already laid out, lay the new item on the old one. Eventually, you will have several piles spread in front of you, some containing just one item, others, several.

3. Consolidate the piles

Next, examine the piles containing only one or two items to see if they can be placed on top of other piles. Sometimes we accidentally put different headings on materials dealing with the same topic. Examining your one- and two-item piles will usually help you to find such items and consolidate your materials.

4. Put the piles in sequence

Spread in front of you now are several piles, each dealing with one topic. Study them and think about what order of topics seems to make sense to you. If you have trouble thinking about it abstractly, find a clear space, and put any pile in it. Now, look at any other pile and ask yourself if that topic should come before or after the first one. If it should come before, then place it to the left of the first pile; if after, place it to the right.

Do the same with a third pile: should it go before the first pile, between the first and second, or after the second? Place it where you think it belongs. Continue this process until you're satisfied that you have them in the sequence you want. You may find that certain materials don't fit into your outline. Set them aside in a pile of their own.

5. Sequence each pile

Now, review each of the other piles and put its contents in the order that makes sense—the first item on top of the pile, the others behind it in sequence.

6. Put the piles in file folders

Next, put each pile in its own file folder, and write the topic word or phrase on the tab. As suggested on p. 35, fasten odd-size materials to a standard sheet of paper for easier handling. Put the pile of materials which didn't fit any classification into its own "Miscellaneous" folder and keep it handy, in case you find that you do need some of the material when you write your presentation. You may also find it useful now to employ the bulletin board method described on page 35.

CATEGORIZE BY MAIN POINTS

A variation of the last method is often helpful when you aren't certain of what to include in your presentation. This can happen when you have so much information that you're at a loss as to how to organize it, or when your presentation has to cover many different points; or when you simply have trouble making an outline. Here are the steps:

1. Think of a slide presentation

First, imagine that you're going to make a slide presentation, in which each of your main points will be highlighted by a slide containing the most important words.

2. Write each main point

Now, write down a summary of each main idea that you think you might want to put on a slide, using a separate sheet for each idea. Imagine that the piece of paper in front of you is actually a slide you'll be projecting for your audience. You don't have to worry about sequencing your ideas now. At this point, just write them in any order they occur to you.

For example, suppose you want to begin your presentation with some background about your organization. As you randomly think of ideas that you might want to talk about, summarize each of them on a sheet of paper. Here are some random ideas that might occur to you, each one followed by a summary that you might write on a separate sheet of paper.

Random idea: We started doing business in 1973.
Write: *Started 1973*

Random idea: Our sales have increased at least 10 percent a year ever since we started.
Write: *10 percent annual increase*

Random idea: Our first product was an electrical timer.
Write: *First product: electrical timer*

Random idea: Harriet Johnson and her husband, Bill Johnson, were the founders.
Write: *Founders: Harriet and Bill Johnson*

Random idea: Their daughter, Melinda, became president last year.
Write: *Melinda president last year*

Random idea: We had a creed from the beginning: "The customer is always right, and we will work together to make sure the customer feels that way."
Write: *Creed: Customer always right. We work together to make sure customer feels that way.*

Random idea: We started out with one employee; now we have 130.
Write: *1973: one employee; today: 130*

3. Spread out the papers

Now you have seven pieces of paper, each with a single idea. Spread them out on your work surface, and shuffle them until they're in an order that makes sense to you. And there's your outline!

SPECIAL SITUATIONS

Multiple notes from one source

Occasionally, you'll find that an article or an interview contains research material that you want to assign to different file folders: one paragraph may be relevant to topic A, another to topic B, and still another to topic C.

Here are some suggestions for doing it efficiently.

1. Identify the passages

Mark each passage clearly by underlining it or circling it, or use a highlighter pen that lays transparent color over the writing. In the margin next to the passage, write an appropriate heading for it, and also write down the page number on which the passage appears.

2. Make a photocopy

Now make a photocopy of all the pages you've marked, and file the original. The reason for making a copy is that you're going to cut apart the paragraphs; retaining the original will be a life-saver if you lose any of the cut-up pieces.

3. Separate the passages

Now cut out each marked paragraph and fasten it to a separate sheet of 8½″ × 11″ paper. The marginal note you've made will tell you which file folder it belongs in.

4. Identify each item

Write down on the sheet of paper the source of the material attached to it. Thus, if it's from a newspaper or magazine or a report, write down the title, the date and the page number. You may want to include this information in your presentation—and few things are more frustrating than being unable to track down the source of an article days or weeks after you've cut it out and filed it.

5. Writing Your Presentation

THREE HELPFUL SUGGESTIONS

Many people find that putting the words on paper is the most difficult part of preparing a presentation. And it *can* be intimidating. You must create a virtual miracle—a written image of what's in your mind that others can understand and respond to.

It's a daunting challenge—but not as daunting as it may at first seem. This chapter will offer a number of suggestions that will help you to write an effective presentation. And the most important suggestion is this: expect to rewrite and rewrite and rewrite. Revising and polishing a presentation makes it more logical, clear, and interesting. Here are some basic suggestions to help you get started in your writing.

Suspend criticism

We seem to have two kinds of mental capacity. One is creative, the other is critical. The creative mind comes up with ideas, and the critical mind evaluates them. Both are necessary when you're writing—but unless you control the critical mind, it can maim or kill the creative.

What often happens is that after we put down a few words or sentences, we start to criticize them. Then we start to rewrite, and we criticize ourselves again. And soon, our critical mind becomes so strong that it virtually overpowers the creative, and we stop, frustrated and discouraged.

Discipline is the solution: when you start to write, don't criticize yourself until you've finished the whole first draft—or at least a major section of your presentation. If you have second thoughts about what you're writing, write down your new thoughts without stopping to correct what's already on paper. Always move forward until you come to a natural stopping point. *Then* let your critical mind go to work and improve what you've written.

Leave lots of room for corrections

You'll find it easier to improve your drafts if you give yourself plenty of room to make corrections. Double-space the lines if you type or if you write in longhand on lined paper; triple-spacing will give you even more room. And leave yourself generous left and right margins—say, one and one-half inches on each side.

Expect to write at least three drafts—and possibly more

Your first draft may be quite rough. The organization may be wrong, the language unclear, the facts irrelevant, and the right information missing. So, think of the first draft as simply a way to put your main points down where you can see them and then refine them.

If you can afford the time, put the draft aside for a day, then return to it when your mind is fresh, and read it again with a more critical eye. Your second draft will be much closer to what you want to say. Again, if there's time, put it away for at least another day, and then correct the weaknesses you find.

While an original draft and two rewrites are a minimum for most people, you can feel perfectly comfortable rewriting three or four times or even more. It will get better each time.

HOW TO BEGIN WRITING

Many people find that the hardest part of writing is the opening sentence, paragraph or idea. Obviously, it's important that it be right, because frequently everything else in the presentation is an elaboration of the opening.

But precisely because the opening *is* so important, we tend to worry excessively about getting it exactly right. And as a result, we have trouble putting down the first words and getting on with the work.

One way to avoid this problem is to forget about the opening until after you've written some or all of the rest of the presentation. Once you've written a couple of pages, you'll have a clearer idea of what the opening words should be. Alternatively, don't write the opening line until after you've finished the whole presentation. By that time, you should know how you want to begin.

Even if you're willing to skip the opening, you may still find that you need a stimulus to get started. One technique is to use nonsense words or sentences for a paragraph or two (for example, "Blah blah blah . . ." or "This and that and this and that and this and that . . .") until you get to a point where you want to begin your actual writing.

Still another way to start is to talk your way into the presentation by dictating your opening words to yourself. That is, say out loud, "What I really want to say is . . ." Now write down what you "really want to say." Voicing your ideas in this way can be quite helpful in keeping your mind on track.

THREE PRINCIPLES OF GOOD WRITING

Accuracy, Brevity, Clarity: these are the ABCs of good presentation writing. Let's see how they can help you to improve your presentation.

How to improve your accuracy

Accuracy applies to the *content* of your presentation—your facts and conclusions. It also applies to your vocabulary, spelling and grammar. So let's consider some suggestions for achieving accuracy in these areas.

Accuracy of your content: One common cause of inaccuracy is careless copying of notes and source materials. We often drop or add words, switch numbers or omit them. The possibilities are almost limitless, so make it a practice to check the material you're quoting to make sure it's right. And then check it again to make sure it's *absolutely* right.

Accuracy of your inferences: A second common cause of inaccuracy is the drawing of unwarranted inferences or conclusions from the evidence. If you are trying to prove a point and your evidence doesn't fully back it up, be cautious about your inferences.

Below are three pairs of phrases. The first in each pair is assertive; the second is more restrained. The assertive one is useful if you're quite certain of your inferences. The restrained one is softer in tone, and, because it sounds reasonable and judicious, may be just as effective, even if your evidence is not quite as strong.

Assertive: We can plainly see that . . .
Restrained: This evidence suggests that . . .

Assertive: There can be no doubt that . . .
Restrained: It would seem fair to conclude that . . .

Assertive: These facts obviously speak for themselves.
Restrained: We can infer from these facts that . . .

Use a familiar vocabulary

Beware of using new words you're not comfortable with. If you use a word incorrectly, those in your audience who know it's wrong will find you less believable, and those who don't know will find you confusing. If you want to use a new word, first check it out with someone who knows its meaning.

How to improve your spelling

If you're delivering your presentation orally and not in writing, accurate spelling is no problem. Of course, if you're using visual aids with words on them, you'll want to make sure they're spelled correctly.

Carelessness is a common cause of spelling errors. You may know the correct spelling, but in writing it down, you may leave out a letter, or put in an extra one, or transpose the order. This tends to happen on large charts or graphs accompanying a presentation.

Another cause of error is simple ignorance. If you're in any doubt about a word, look it up in the dictionary, or ask a good speller to review your presentation for misspellings. Dictionaries of commonly misspelled words are available, but they're of limited use unless you already know the correct spelling. More helpful are dictionaries which list commonly misspelled words in the ways in which they're commonly misspelled (such as the *Webster's Spell It Right Dictionary*, published by Perigee Books).

Another way to improve your spelling is to make a list of words that give you trouble. Putting them on small cards will enable you to keep them alphabetized. The following list (taken from my book *Successful Business Writing*, published by Perigee Books) is a handy compilation of frequently misspelled words:

absence	choose	dining
accept	chosen	disappear
accident	coming	disappoint
accidentally	commit	dividend
accommodate	commitment	doesn't
acknowledgment	committed	don't
acquaint	committee	during
acquaintance	committing	
across	competition	
affect	complete	effect
aggravate	comptroller	eighth
all right	conscientious	embarrass
amateur	conscious	environment
appearance	consensus	equipment
argument	convenience	equipped
around	convenient	escape
athletic	coolly	exaggerate
auxiliary	council	excellent
	counsel	excite
beginning	criticize	excitement
believe	criticism	exciting
believed		exercise
beneficial	deceive	existence
benefit	decide	experiment
benefited	decision	
buoyant	definite	
business	descend	familiar
busy	descendant *or*	fascinate
	descendent	February
capital	describe	finally
career	description	foreign
catalog	desert	foreigners
cemetery	dessert	forth
certain	develop	forty
character	difference	four
chief	different	friend

glamorous
glamor
government
grammar
grievance

hadn't
height
hero
heroes
heroine
humor
humorous

image
imaginary
imagination
imagine
immediate
immediately
individual
interest
interested
it's (contraction)
its (possessive)

judgment

knowledge
knowledgeable

laboratory
latter
literature
lonely
loose
lose
losing

maintenance
marriage

marries
marry
meant
mischievous
monetary
municipal

necessary
necessity
noticeable

occasion
occasionally
occur
occurred
occurrence
occurring
o'clock
omitted
opinion
opportunity

parallel
parliament
performance
perhaps
personal
personnel
pleasant
possess
precede
prejudice
president
principal
principle
probably
proceed
professor
promissory
promotional
pronunciation

prophecy (noun)
prophesy (verb)
purchasable

quiet
quite

receive
recommend
referred
regrettable
relieve
responsibility
restaurant
rhythm

salable *or*
    saleable
schedule
seize
sense
separate
shining
similar
simplify
society
speech
stationary (still)
stationery (paper, etc.)
stop
stopped
stopping
strength
studied
studies
study
studying
succeed
success
successful
superintendent

supersede	too	Wednesday
surprise	tragedy	weird
	transferred	where
technicality	transient	whether
tendency	tries	woman
than	tried	writ
then	truly	writer
their	two	writing
there		written
they're	until	
thousandth		yield
to	villain	you're
together		your

A few words about brevity

You can generally shorten anything you've written without losing the meaning. What's more, shortening usually makes it easier to understand. If you wait at least a day, you'll generally find it easier to eliminate words, phrases and sometimes whole paragraphs. The following two paragraphs illustrate the benefits of editing.

How to achieve clarity

Clarity in writing is like success in love. It comes more easily to some than to others, but with practice, everyone improves. Below are some techniques to help you attain clarity.

Read aloud: If your presentation is not highly technical, reading it aloud to someone who knows nothing about the subject can be useful. Ask the person to stop you whenever a thought or a sentence is unclear. If you can clarify it to your listener, your ultimate audience will understand it.

OTHER WAYS TO IMPROVE YOUR WRITING

Use active verbs

Most verbs have an active and a passive form. Here are some pairs of sentences using the same verbs in passive and active forms.

| Passive: | The situation is understood. |
| Active: | I understand the situation. |

| Passive: | It was given our full attention. |
| Active: | We gave it our full attention. |

| Passive: | The challenge will be undertaken. |
| Active: | We will undertake the challenge. |

| Passive: | The future can be seen clearly. |
| Active: | We see the future clearly. |

The active form makes a sentence livelier and more interesting to the audience, so it's a good idea to use it whenever possible. When you edit your first draft, make passive verbs active wherever you can. (There are exceptions, a notable one being doctoral dissertations, where the passive voice is often not only tolerated, but, alas, actively encouraged.)

Shun "-tion"

Compare the following pairs:

> The sales force has a lot of *motivation*.
> The sales force is well *motivated*.

> The group began taking *action* immediately.
> The group began to *act* immediately.

> One of our first priorities is *reorganization* of the department.
> One of our first priorities is to *reorganize* the department.

A sentence will be more vigorous if it uses a verb rather than a noun ending in "-tion" which stands for a verb. When you edit your presentation, see if you can replace "-tion" words with verbs.

Keep sentences short

Shorter sentences are easier to understand than longer ones. For example:

> You'll be associating with a group of experienced professionals all of whom enjoy their work and take pride in their individual contributions to their projects, which is a major reason why we have grown nearly 20 percent in the last twelve months.

Using shorter sentences, the paragraph might read:

> You'll be associating with a group of experienced professionals. All of them enjoy their work and take pride in their individual contributions to their projects. Our staff is a major reason we have grown nearly 20 percent in the last twelve months.

There is no absolutely right length for a sentence, but if you make a habit of keeping sentences less than two lines long, you'll insure that your audience can follow them easily.

Use transitions

Transitional words and phrases can help your sentences and your ideas flow more smoothly. Here's an example:

> We plan to meet them tomorrow. We do not know yet what the results will be.

There is an abruptness between the two sentences, which vanishes when you insert a single transitional word:

> We plan to meet them tomorrow. But we do not know yet what the results will be.

The "But" helps to link the second sentence to the first. This kind of transition is natural and customary when we're speaking, but we tend to neglect it in writing. Think about whether you can improve your writing by inserting more transitions. Common transitional words and phrases include:

> And . . .
> But . . .
> So . . .
> Moreover . . ./What's more . . .
> In addition . . ./Additionally . . .
> Further . . .
> On the one hand . . ./On the other hand . . .
> This suggests that . . .
> From this, we can see that . . .
> For example . . ./For instance . . .
> As a case in point . . .

Use paragraphs and subheads

There is something forbidding about a solid page of print in a presentation. It tends to look like an endless and difficult desert.

The solution is to break up the pages with paragraphs and subheads. Generally, once a paragraph grows to more than eight or ten lines, it's time to think of breaking it up into two paragraphs. For additional visual variation, use deeply indented paragraphs, like those on page 46.

The small titles you see before each new subject in this chapter are subheads. They serve as the reader's guideposts in following the presentation. What's more, they tease the reader's interest: when you see a subhead, you want to know more about the subject.

More about subheads: Consider the type of subhead that begins this paragraph. A subhead which is on the same line as the paragraph it's introducing is particularly useful for emphasizing several subordinate ideas under a major subhead.

Use examples

Whenever you make a general statement, try to follow it with an example of what you mean. Here, for example, is a general statement:

> We all know about the problem of children with learning disabilities. But we are just beginning to deal with the problem of adults with learning disabilities.

The following sentence illustrates the statement:

> It's been estimated that between 10 and 20 percent of all adults—some twenty-five to fifty million people—are learning disabled and yet there is not one organization in this country to help them.

For other illustrations of when and how to provide concrete examples, read any two or three pages of this book; you'll find a multitude of general statements followed by concrete examples.

When to use quotation marks

Some writers put quotation marks around words or phrases to which they want to call attention. Two typical examples are:

- To emphasize a word: We are looking forward to working on this "unique" project.
- To show that the writer is using a slang phrase: There are three reasons for taking this "with a grain of salt."

Both practices mark the writer as unskilled. Quotation marks are appropriate:

- To enclose direct quotations: "Do you," she asked, "want one lump or two?"
- To enclose titles of articles, book chapters, essays, short stories and poems and musical compositions: "The Physics of Chemistry" is the second chapter in the book.
  "The Magic Flute" is one of my favorite operas.
- To enclose words spoken of as words, or words used in a special sense: The words "up" and "down" have different meanings, depending on their context.
  To computer users, "digital" does not refer to fingers.

Instead of quotation marks, the words can be underlined, e.g.:

> The words <u>up</u> and <u>down</u> have different meanings, depending on their context.

Watch your gender

In recent years, many writers have started using gender-neutral constructions to replace male-oriented sentences.

A person should remember his license plate number.

Gender-neutral variations:

A person should remember his or her license plate number.
We should remember our license plate numbers.
You should remember your license plate number.

If anyone has forgotten, let me remind him . . .

Gender-neutral variations:

Let me remind anyone who has forgotten . . .
If you have forgotten, let me remind you . . .
If anyone has forgotten, let me remind her or him (or "him or her") . . .

While gender neutrality is probably ignored at least as often as it's observed—especially in scientific writing—it is an issue about which more and more men and women are sensitive. If you want to avoid offending anyone, consider gender neutrality.

Avoid "All of you"

In a written or oral presentation, avoid the phrase "All of you," as in:

I know that all of you are interested in what we're going to learn today.

Instead, say simply:

I know that you are interested in what we're going to learn today.

Saying "All of you" suggests that you're speaking to the *group*. However, your listeners are not thinking of themselves as a group; they think of themselves as individuals. When you say "you" rather than "all of you," each member of your audience feels that you are speaking directly to him or her as an individual, rather than to the whole group indiscriminately.

6. Designing a Persuasive Written Presentation

A good-looking written presentation will always make a favorable first impression on the reader, while one that's untidy or thoughtlessly put together may undermine all your efforts, regardless of how worthwhile the contents. In this chapter, we'll discuss how to put together a professional-looking presentation.

APPEARANCE ON THE PAGE

Let's begin by listing some basic ways to improve the appearance of a standard written presentation.

Use a typewriter: If possible, write the presentation on a typewriter. Handwritten presentations rarely get the attention or respect given those done on a typewriter.

A note to computer users and potential users: The inferior print quality of even the best current dot matrix printers gives an impression that the writer is satisfied with less than the best. If making the best possible impression is important to you, use only letter quality printing.

Spacing between the lines: In general, double-spaced presentations look better than single-spaced; it's a good idea to use double-spacing if your presentation is to be persuasive as well as informative.

Another factor to consider is the length of your presentation. If it's a straightforward, factual report of not more than three or four pages, single-spacing may be perfectly satisfactory. If, on the other hand, you want a more elegant and weighty look, double-spacing will do a better job for you.

Give yourself generous margins: Wide margins look better than narrow margins. At a minimum, your left and right margins should be one inch wide. Many professional presentations have margins of about 1½″ on the left, and 2″ on the right.

White space at the top and bottom should also be generous. Figure on at least 1½″, and consider going up to 2″ for upper and lower margins.

Select your paragraphing style: Earlier, we suggested that frequent paragraphs help to make a presentation easier to read. One way of indicating paragraphs is to indent the first line four or five spaces. For a more distinctive appearance, try indenting ten or fifteen spaces.

Another way to indicate paragraphs is to double the space between the end of one paragraph and the beginning of the next. That is, to double-space if the page is single-spaced, and to quadruple-space if the page is double-spaced.

Still another way is to indent *and* to double the space between the lines. Personal preference is your best guide in choosing one of these designs.

The value of page numbering: Numbering the pages helps to insure that you've included all of them when you hand out the presentation. Page-numbering also makes it easier for the reader to find information. Put page numbers at the top or the bottom, as you prefer. They are usually centered, although if they're at the top, they are sometimes put at the right margin. For a slightly more elegant look, instead of simply indicating the page number by a numeral, write "page 1," (or whatever the number).

In longer presentations, the pages with the introduction or preface are frequently numbered with small Roman numerals: i, ii, iii, etc.

Should you justify? Justified copy has a straight margin down the page; it's the style most newspapers and books follow for right and left margins. Unjustified copy has a ragged edge; on typewritten pages, the left margin is justified but the right side is usually unjustified. Justification of both margins is achieved by adding equal space between letters and words to fill out the line. All word processors and many electronic typewriters justify. The question is, should you take advantage of this option?

For a typewritten presentation, I recommend that you don't justify, because justification tends to look fussy: it calls attention to itself. A good-looking presentation should look neat, but not gaudy, and justified typewritten copy looks a bit gaudy.

USE HELPFUL INTRODUCTORY ELEMENTS

Reading a presentation for the first time is like being introduced to strangers at a party. If they seem welcoming, you want to know them better. Similarly, if the introduction of your written presentation is welcoming, the reader will want to know more about what's inside. For a typewritten presentation, this means that the beginning clearly suggests what the reader can expect to find inside. Here are some suggestions for welcoming the reader.

The short presentation: For a short presentation of, say, under five pages, you'll usually need only a brief explanation at the top of the first page about who the presentation is from, who it's addressed to, and what it's about. It's also a good idea to date it. Here's a common format for business and professional presentations, followed by some explanatory comments:

June 1, 1987

From: Sydney Smith
To: The Executive Committee
Subject: Pension plan recommendations

Introduction

About three months ago, the executive committee asked me to review our existing pension plan and to recommend improvements . . .

The "To" line: This is not always necessary; if you think it will be useful, include this line. Otherwise, omit it.

The "Subject" line: The purpose of this line is to give the reader a quick idea of the main topic of your presentation. Some people like to capitalize each of the major words on this line (e.g., "Pension Plan Recommendations"), but the trend is toward less capitalization.

The heading "Introduction": While this heading is not necessary, it does give the reader a sense of the presentation's importance, adding psychological weight to your ideas.

The longer presentation: Presentations longer than four or five pages usually deserve a separate title page. (For that matter, there's no reason why two- or three-page presentations can't be dressed up with a separate title page.) Here are a couple of representative title pages:

Pension Plan Recommendations

A Report to the Executive Committee

from

Sidney Smith

June 1, 1987

A Proposal to the Excel Corporation
for the
Annual Sales Meeting

June 1, 1987

Sidney Smith Associates
Smith Plaza
Oaklawn, MA 00001

(123) 456–7890

Alternatively, if the first page is on an organization's letterhead, the writer's identification ("Sidney Smith Associates") obviously can be omitted.

Note that in one of these examples the text is underlined, in the other it is not. Both are equally acceptable.

INCLUDE A TABLE OF CONTENTS

If you have fewer than four or five major headings or topics, a table of contents may not be too useful. But if there are more than that, the table will add another professional touch to your presentation. Here's a typical format for a table of contents, followed by explanatory comments:

Subordinate topics: The table lists not only the major topics, e.g., "Introduction," "I. The Basic Facts," but also the subordinate topics, which are the main subheads in the presentation. This makes the table look more substantial, and it can also help the reader grasp the overall thrust of your presentation.

Dotted lines: The dotted lines between the topic and the page number are a personal choice. Often, they're omitted.

Spacing: Note that while each Roman numeral has one more character than the one above it, the first words following the numerals all line up vertically. This makes for a neater appearance.

Charts and Graphs: Listing them separately in the table of contents is a further aid to the reader, and, of course, makes the table of contents more impressive.

PRESENTING CHARTS, GRAPHS AND OTHER MATERIALS

Keep in mind that graphic illustrations—charts, graphs and other nontext materials—are simply another form of written communication: the sentence as picture. When you plan to use a graph or chart, ask yourself: does it clearly describe the point I want to make? Here are some things you can do to help the reader understand your graphics.

Refer to it in the text: Your text should identify the graphic so that the reader can quickly refer to it. The most common way to identify graphics is Figure 1, Figure 2 (or Fig. 1, Fig. 2), or Chart 1, Chart 2.

Label clearly: Label each graphic clearly so that the reader can understand its purpose at a glance. The label can be on the graphic or adjacent to it as part of the caption. But wherever it is, it should give a clear idea of what the graphic illustrates. For example, Figure 1 shows a chart which will leave most readers baffled. Figure 2 is the same chart with a caption. And Figure 3 is the same chart with a caption and a title on the chart.

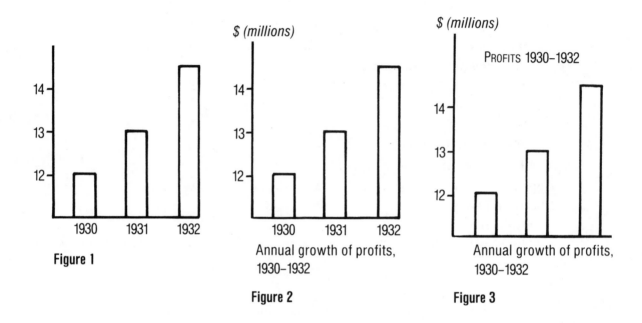

Figure 1

Annual growth of profits, 1930–1932

Figure 2

Annual growth of profits, 1930–1932

Figure 3

Choose the right graphics: Think about the main point you want your chart to illustrate, and then select the format that will illustrate that point most clearly. For example, a single-line graph (Figure 4) clearly illustrates changes over a period of time. A graph with two or more lines (Figure 5) is useful for comparing changes in more than one factor over a period of time.

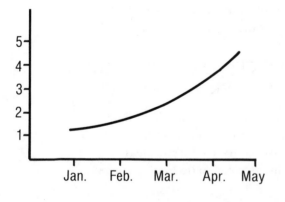

Figure 4

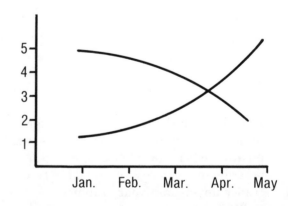

Figure 5

A bar chart (Figure 6) is often a more dramatic way to present the same information as a line graph—the bars have an assertiveness lacking in the line. Twin bars (Figure 7) illustrate the changes in two factors over a period of time. But if you want to compare more than two factors, a line graph is usually easier to interpret than a bar chart.

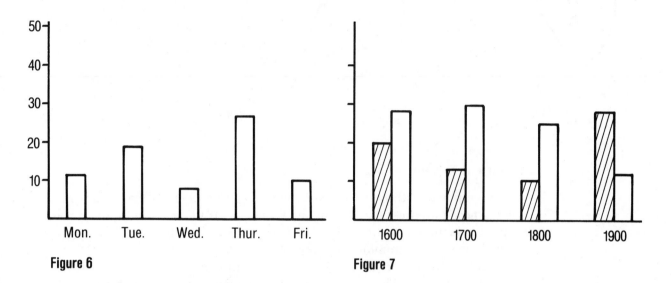

Figure 6

Figure 7

A segmented bar chart (Figure 8) will illustrate components of the totals you're describing.

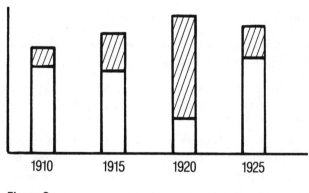

Figure 8

Pie charts are also commonly used to illustrate components of a whole (Figure 9). And they can also show changes in totals over a period of time (Figure 10).

Placing the graphics: Locate your graphics where the reader can find them easily—generally, as close as possible to the text that refers to them. The reader can quickly find a chart that immediately follows the text. If it falls elsewhere on the page or on a facing page it will be a bit less convenient. And if it's on a following page, as Figures 9 and 10 are, or in a different section of the presentation, it will be still less convenient.

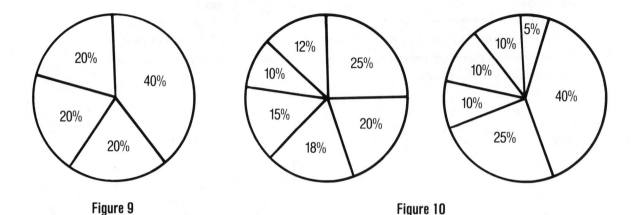

Figure 9   **Figure 10**

Statistical tables

As with graphic illustrations, statistical tables can be thought of as visual sentences, whose purpose—like that of any sentence—is to convey information. If you plan to include statistical tables in your presentation, the following suggestions will help you communicate more clearly.

Refer to the table in the text: Your text should identify the table so that the reader can quickly refer to it. The most common way to identify tables is Table 1, Table 2, and so on.

> As Table 1 indicates, we have been progressing much better in the Middle West than in the East and South.

Or, more fully, you might mention the title of the table as well.

> We have been progressing much better in the Middle West than in the East and the South (Table 1: Regional Sales Totals).

It goes without saying that the caption for the statistical table itself should indicate the table number and the title. (See "Write clear titles and captions" below.)

Eliminate unessentials: Just as good writing eliminates inessential words, so a good statistical table will eliminate unnecessary data. Review your tables to make sure that they contain only the information necessary for your reader to understand the points that you're trying to make.

Write clear titles and captions: Your reader will understand your statistical tables more easily if you label them clearly. At the very least, each table should have a number and a title:

> Table 1: Net Profit for Selected Retailers

You may also want to add a caption which will succinctly explain the significance of the table, or which calls the reader's attention to your main point:

> Table 4: World-Wide Tennis Ball Production
> Production has increased substantially in all parts of the world in the last decade, but the most pronounced increases have been in Asia and Toledo.

BINDING YOUR PRESENTATION

If your presentation is only three or four pages long, you probably won't want— or need—to bind it in a special cover. But if it's longer than that, a cover will be a useful, easy, inexpensive way to dress it up. Your stationery store offers a variety of choices. Here's a list of some you'll want to consider:

Punchless report covers: They are called "punchless" because no holes need be punched in the pages to bind them in place. Simply insert your sheets into the cover and slide a rigid plastic backbone over the fold to clamp them in place. The pages can easily be changed.

These binders hold a packet of paper about ⅛″ thick; depending on paper thickness, this is sixteen to twenty 8½″ × 11″ sheets. Punchless report covers come in both opaque and transparent flexible plastic, in a variety of colors.

Punched-paper report covers: These bind the papers in place by metal prongs, which allow pages to be changed. Some will hold up to a ½″ stack of 8½″ × 11″ paper; others, up to 3″; and some, as high as 6″. They are available with prongs along either the 8½″ or the 11″ side.

They come in a variety of colors and styles, including pressboard, transparent plastic, and opaque plastic with and without clear windows through which the title can be read. The pressboard is rigid, the plastic flexible.

Portfolios: Portfolios are binders with pockets on the inside of one or both covers. Some also have metal prongs so that you can bind punched paper in them. Others have leaves of clear plastic into which you can insert your material. Portfolios are useful when you have different sizes of paper which cannot conveniently be bound together.

Ring binders: Those with rigid covers can easily be stored upright; flexible covers are lighter and fit more compactly in briefcases and drawers. Binders come with between two and seven rings, three-ring being the most common for 8½″ × 11″ paper. (Another type is multiring, whose rings are spaced about ¾″ apart.) Ring diameters generally range from 1″ to 3″; figure about fifty sheets for each ¼″ of ring size.

Display books: Binders with plastic sleeves that hold and protect paper and other display material. These are used mainly for repeated presentations, as, for example, on sales calls, where the buyers are expected to look at the printed material, but not to keep it.

Easel binders: These have a front cover that hinges back and forms a support, permitting the binder to stand by itself on a flat surface. They're popular for presentations to one or two people sitting across a table from the presenter, who can flip each page without having to worry about keeping the binder open and the pages visible.

Index Tabs

If your printed presentation has several sections, consider using index tab sheets to separate them. The sheets are of light cardboard, with tabs that project about ⅓″ beyond the sheet. Some tabs are preprinted with numbers or letters; others are blank; still others are transparent plastic sleeves into which you can slip your own titles.

SELECTING PAPER

The paper you use in your presentation can affect its reception: good paper makes the presentation look more authoritative. Here are some basic facts about paper.

Papers are made of cotton fibers, chemical fibers, or a combination of the two. The greater the cotton content, the better the appearance, permanence and erasability. Paper made from cotton fibers is called "rag content paper" and usually carries a watermark—which you can see when you hold it up to the light—as a sign of quality. 100 percent rag paper is made only of cotton fiber; 75 percent, 50 percent and 25 percent rag have proportionally less rag content.

The standard size of sheets is 8½″ × 11″. Legal size paper, also called "cap size," is 8½ × 13″ or 14″, varying in different parts of the country.

While you can buy paper in smaller packets of 100 sheets, you'll save quite a bit of money by buying a ream—500 sheets. The label on the package will indicate any rag content and also the paper's "substance." Substance is based on the weight of 500 sheets of 17″ × 22″ paper. So, if 500 17″ × 22″ sheets of the paper in this book weigh 16 lbs., it will be designated as 16-lb. substance. The lightest papers in general use are 9-lb. substance, the heaviest, 20-lb. Use 20-lb. substance rag bond paper for a very good-looking presentation. "Bond paper" was used originally for printing bonds and other important documents, and now refers to high quality typewriter paper. (If you want to make even more of an impression, textured papers are available at premium prices.)

MAKING COPIES

It goes without saying that if you are making multiple copies of a written presentation, all should be as clear as the original. However, you may want to distinguish some copies from others. For example, you may want to give the highest-ranking member of the group a copy with a more prestigious binding to show that you appreciate his or her importance. This is a delicate psychological point, and the best way to decide is to think about your individual situation, and whether a special copy will help you.

7. Making an Effective Oral Presentation

THE FIRST, SECOND AND THIRD RULES

Practice. Practice. Practice. Those are the first, second and third rules of successful oral presentations. If you're like most people, you'll feel at least a flutter of nervousness when you speak before an audience. But if you've rehearsed adequately, you'll get control of your nerves much faster, and you'll feel better and do better. Eventually, you may even enjoy having people listen to you and learn from you.

ALLOW TIME FOR REHEARSALS

Just as actors spend weeks rehearsing a play, it's a good idea to space your practice periods over several days, rather than wait until the last few hours before you have to give the presentation. Giving yourself extra time will fix the words and the speech rhythms more firmly in your mind. Further, it will give you more of an opportunity to edit and improve your remarks.

Of course, sometimes you may have only a day or two to prepare. In that case, try to arrange your schedule so that you can rehearse two or three times over a period of several hours. Most people find that reviewing a presentation at intervals gives better results than concentrating all the rehearsals into one period.

DUPLICATE THE ENVIRONMENT

If you can, rehearse in an environment like the one where you'll deliver your presentation. The ideal environment is the actual room itself. This will enable you to become familiar with the peculiarities of the space—the lighting, the acoustics, the placement of the audience, etc.

If that's not possible, the next best thing is an environment similar to it. If your presentation will be in a large hall, try to find another large hall to practice in. If it's a small office, or a conference room, see if you can find similar rehearsal space.

DUPLICATE THE POSTURE

Since one purpose of rehearsing is to come as close as possible to the conditions of the presentation, try to duplicate the posture that you'll assume when you make your presentation.

If you'll be standing at a lectern when you speak, rehearse by standing at a lectern or a table. If you'll be sitting across a desk or a conference table from your audience, rehearse it that way. This will help you to think about such physical circumstances as sitting comfortably, or demonstrating a piece of equipment. As you rehearse, consider these details:

- Are your notes arranged so that you can refer to them quickly?
- Can you turn the pages easily?
- If you plan to refer to charts or graphs or to demonstrate something such as a piece of equipment, is it placed so that you can reach it and demonstrate it comfortably?

PRACTICING YOUR PRESENTATION

What's the best way to make a presentation? To read it to your audience? To deliver it from memory? To speak from notes or from an outline?

In fact, all are equally good methods. All are simply means to an end: to make your audience feel you're speaking to each of them individually. And if you can make that contact best by reading rather than by memorizing, then reading is the best method for you. If you make contact better with a memorized speech—that's the way to go. Let's consider some points to keep in mind for each of these techniques.

Speaking from a script

Speaking from a script is both the safest and the riskiest way to deliver a presentation. It's safe because your material is always in front of you to refer to. It's risky because you may keep your eyes focused on the words you're reading, and forget to make contact with the audience. To increase the safety and decrease the risk, start rehearsing by reading the presentation aloud several times. As you rehearse, keep the following points in mind:

Read it for clarity

First, read your remarks aloud to see how they feel in your mouth. You may find that certain word combinations, while they read easily, are difficult to pronounce aloud clearly. For example, when one word ends, and the next begins, with the same letter, the two words tend to run together—e.g., "less sympathy," "read downward," "rush shamelessly"—and your listeners may not understand exactly what you're saying.

One remedy for the problem: use different words that are easier to say, e.g., "not as much sympathy" for "less sympathy." Another remedy: mark the script with a symbol to remind yourself to pronounce distinctly. For example, insert a vertical line between two words that run together. Use a colored marker to insure that you'll see it.

Read it for rhythm

In our normal conversation, we vary the speed and the pitch of our voices. If we're excited, we speak faster. If we're angry we often speak louder—or softer—than normal. And when we ask a question, doesn't our voice rise at the end of the sentence? All of these variations make our words more interesting to our listeners. In contrast, to describe a voice that speaks in an unvarying monotone, we use the adjective—monotonous.

So, read your presentation through at least once in order to think about how to vary the tone from sentence to sentence. Here are some variations you can introduce:

Insert pauses

A pause is an excellent way to get people to pay attention to you. For example, just before you begin, if you pause for two or three seconds, your listeners will focus on you, wondering what you're going to say. Subconsciously, they'll be asking themselves, "What's the reason for the delay?" And as soon as you start, they'll feel relieved that you're communicating with them.

Plan to insert pauses throughout your presentation. Consider making a short pause between each sentence, and a slightly longer pause between paragraphs. Not only does this help your audience to focus, it also allows them to follow your thinking more easily.

If you think you'll forget about pausing when you make your presentation, insert the word "Pause" or a symbol at the appropriate places to remind yourself.

Ask questions

Normally, when you speak, the audience remains fairly passive: all they have to do is listen. Unfortunately, this makes it easier for their minds to wander. Asking them questions periodically is a good way to bring them back to you.

Make your questions short. And follow them up with an answer, so that the audience follows along with you easily as you speak. For example, suppose after you've made your opening remarks, you state your main topic:

> In the next few minutes, I'd like to discuss the main problems now facing us.

You can turn it into an attention-getting question by phrasing it:

> What are the main problems facing us now? That's what I'd like to discuss in the next few minutes.

Another example: suppose, toward the end of the presentation, you plan to issue a call for action, and you've written:

Here is what I think we should do.

In delivering it, you might say:

What should we do? Here is how I believe we should proceed.

To make your remarks even more interesting, remember to pause after asking your question. This will force your audience to think about what you're saying. Then, when you continue, you'll put them at ease because you'll be providing them with the solution.

How often should you ask a question? In a ten- to twenty-minute presentation, you can generally put in three or four to good effect.

Maintain eye contact

If someone looks at you frequently in a private conversation, you feel he or she is interested in you. But if the person looks away, avoiding eye contact, you usually feel uncomfortable—as if you're being excluded.

Similarly, maintaining eye contact is essential to keep an audience actively interested. Techniques for maintaining eye contact may vary with the size of your audience.

For an audience of one, simply look at that person as often as you can. This tends to be a bit difficult when you're reading from a paper, because you have to keep looking down at your notes, thus breaking contact.

That's why rehearsal is so important. The more familiar you become with your written presentation, the more secure you'll feel about looking up from the printed page and speaking directly to your listener.

To remind yourself to maintain eye contact, write a symbol such as an eye, or make a note such as "LOOK UP" in the margin of your presentation. Try to do this at least once for every five or six lines of your presentation.

Also, always make eye contact when you're asking a question. This makes the audience feel that you are really expecting them to think about an answer. For example, in the following passage, you'd make a point of looking at the listener when you were speaking the lines enclosed in brackets.

. . . I believe that once I explain the reasons behind our decision, you'll probably agree that these recommendations make sense.

[Now, what are those reasons? That's what I'd like to explore with you for the next few moments.]

To begin, there is the fact that our department is now running at a deficit of some $5,000 a year . . .

If you're speaking to a relatively small audience, say, up to fifteen or twenty people, try to look at all of them periodically. If you're all seated at a large conference table, scan everybody from time to time. Sometimes you might look only to those on your left, sometimes only to the right, and sometimes you'll sweep both left and right.

Many listeners tend to be touchy about this: if they sense you're looking at others but not at them, they'll feel you think they're not worthy of attention, and they'll be resentful. You can prevent this simply by remembering to look at everyone.

One political note: Often when you're making a presentation to a small group, one member of the audience will be more important than the others—it may be the boss, or the senior delegate, or simply the one who carries the most influence. Make eye contact with that person more than with the others. This will usually earn his or her good will for two reasons: it shows that you respect the person's seniority, and confirms his or her importance to the rest of the audience.

When you're speaking to larger groups, say, more than twenty-five people, it's difficult to maintain eye contact with everyone. You'll usually find that a large number of people will not be looking at you. This doesn't necessarily mean they're not interested in what you're saying, but it can be discouraging if you interpret it that way.

The solution is to scan the audience until you find two or three or four people in different parts of the room who *are* looking at you with interest. Then, as you speak, talk directly to them, first to one, then to another. This will help you feel that you're making person-to-person contact. Consequently, it will strengthen the conviction and persuasiveness of everything you say.

Practice demonstrations

Suppose your presentation requires you to demonstrate something, like a new piece of machinery, or a dance step, or the correct sequence for throwing a series of switches. Be sure to rehearse until you can do it clearly and automatically, so that the audience will understand exactly what you're demonstrating.

For example, if you are demonstrating to several people, there's a chance that some of them may miss it the first time. So, after you've finished your first demonstration, consider repeating it, saying something like:

> In case some of you didn't see exactly how that went, let me go through it for you once again.

You may also find it helpful to watch TV commercials closely. The pitchmen are generally expert at demonstrating their products and services. Watching how they gesture, how they move their hands, how they use their voices to emphasize certain points, may give you valuable ideas for your own presentation. (In chapter 9, "Using Visual Aids in Oral Presentations," you'll find more helpful suggestions that you may be able to adapt for improving your demonstrations.)

Certainly, it's a good idea to rehearse in front of a mirror, so that you can watch yourself and improve your performance. If you can, rehearse in front of another person whose opinion you respect, and ask for objective opinions about what was not clear, or how you can improve. And if you have access to a video camera, use it to record your practice demonstrations so that you can see more clearly what you're doing, and how you might better your performance.

Gestures

A certain liveliness in your gestures can enhance the persuasiveness of your oral presentation. The important question, of course, is: What's appropriate for *you?*

If you're normally an undemonstrative person, or one who avoids dramatic gestures, then you'd probably feel uncomfortable using them in your presentation. Nevertheless, because they can help you to be a more interesting speaker, try practicing a few in front of a mirror, and use them to the extent that you can feel natural with them.

On the other hand, if you tend to be highly physical when talking to people, you might ask yourself whether it's appropriate for your presentation, or whether you should tone it down.

While there are no absolute rules here, gestures and changes in facial expression will generally enhance your presentation. Practice them in front of a mirror, and then, when you rehearse your presentation, indicate with symbols or words which gestures you should use at which points. Here are a few simple ones to consider:

The enumerating finger: When you're listing points, e.g., "First . . . second . . . third . . ." hold up your hand and raise the same number of fingers.

A consideration to keep in mind about gestures is the size of your audience. Before a small audience around a conference table, large movements will seem overly dramatic; so make your gestures less pronounced than you would before a large audience. For example, when enumerating for a small audience, you might raise your hand off the table only two or three inches; before a large audience, you might bring your whole arm upwards.

The total embrace: When you're discussing a total quantity, for example:

> *Everyone* in our company is dedicated to the idea of service . . .

or,

> Take a look at *all* of this data, and what does it add up to?

extend both arms partly forward, palms slightly upturned, as if you were carrying a large bowl.

The urgent fist: The fist is a symbol of force or power. If you're expressing an idea that contains such imagery, a fist will help vivify it. For instance, speak any of these phrases with and without making a fist and notice the difference in the forcefulness of your words:

> We are going to succeed . . .
> This is a terrific challenge . . .
> The numbers are absolutely clear.

The variety of possible gestures is probably infinite. What's important is for you to understand that they can enhance your spoken words, and to practice them until you feel quite comfortable using them.

Facial expressions

Like gestures, facial expressions can make your oral presentation more interesting. A case in point: When you start, a genuine smile will make your audience feel that you're happy to be there—and they'll respond with more attention. When you ask a question, you'll again get more attention if you raise your eyebrows quizzically, as most people do in casual conversation. If you remember to smile at intervals throughout your presentation, it will help your audience to relax, to feel that you like them, that you're at ease with them, and that they can listen to you, not as a lecturer, but as a friend.

BEGINNING YOUR PRESENTATION

Chapter 2 suggested various ways to begin your presentation. But in certain circumstances, it may be useful to make some informal comments to set the audience at ease, before going into your prepared remarks.

When you're meeting with a small group, these introductory remarks serve essentially as a bridge between the informal chatter that occurred while everyone was settling down, and your prepared presentation.

The remarks can be brief and businesslike: "If you're ready, we'll begin," or "I think we're all set now. Shall we start?"

If it's appropriate, you may want to introduce a bit of informal enthusiasm: "We have some exciting ideas to share with you, and if you're ready, so are we."

Or you may want to explain how you plan to handle the presentation:

> Before we begin, I'd like to explain how we plan to divide the labor between us. First, I'll go through the background with you. Then Alice will discuss the engineering aspects. Norm will cover the legal side. And I'll finish up with a summary of the major points.

If you feel comfortable making casually humorous remarks at this point, by all means do so. (See section on humor, page 68.)

PROVIDING A WRITTEN COPY

A question to ask yourself before giving your presentation is: Should I provide the audience with a written copy of my remarks?

Generally, if you do give people a written copy, they will read ahead of you, so that they're barely listening to you at all. For this reason, it's a good idea to avoid distributing copies until after you've finished your presentation. And it's a courtesy to explain this in advance, so that people will know whether or not to take notes:

> Feel free to make notes, but we will pass out copies of our proposal after the presentation, so that you can study it at your leisure.

If your presentation covers a number of subjects, and you're worried about whether your audience will be able to follow it all, you can give them a brief outline of your major topics. It's helpful if you explain the outline:

I'd like to give you an outline of our remarks so that you can follow us easily from topic to topic.

In a large meeting, if you decide to distribute the outline, you'll have to do it in advance, to avoid taking up an inordinate amount of time. But in a small meeting, you have a number of options, each of which involves some subtle emotional factors to think about.

One option is for the main speaker to distribute copies of the outline at the start of the meeting. In this case, the speaker becomes, as it were, the giver of a gift, and enjoys the good feeling that accrues to anyone who offers a present.

If more than one person will be involved in making the presentation, the main speaker can ask one of the others to distribute the outline. This gives the main speaker an aura of authority, because he or she has the power to order someone else to carry out an activity. Obviously, this is a useful technique for establishing the importance of the main speaker.

Still a third technique is to distribute the outline before the meeting begins, so that the listeners have copies in front of them as soon as they sit down. This creates an impression of good, businesslike planning.

WHEN MORE THAN ONE PERSON IS PRESENTING

You may find yourself in a situation in which more than one person is making a presentation. A typical example: when you and two or three colleagues are making a proposal to another group—say, to another department, or to a prospective customer. At these times, your meeting will be more professional if you remember to do two things:

Introduce your team: When two groups of people come together for a meeting, there is usually some informal banter before the meeting begins. During these first few minutes, introductions are made more or less haphazardly. Once the meeting begins, the leader of those who are making the presentation should formally introduce each colleague, and in a brief phrase or two, describe the reason the person is there:

Marjorie's our legal counsel and will explain the fine print . . .

Harold is in charge of our printing operations, and he's the perfect person to answer your question in that area.

This courtesy makes each of your people stand out as an individual with something useful to contribute, and it satisfies the other group's curiosity about who the members of your team are.

Plan on the presenters: It's a good idea to think in advance about whether one or more of you should do the talking. If your presentation is more than about ten minutes long, consider having more than one person talk. The reason: All other things being equal, a second speaker creates a change of pace that frequently helps to increase the listener's attention.

Naturally, all other things are *not* always equal. In general, it makes sense to avoid using a poor speaker. One exception: A poor speaker can still be very persuasive if he or she has specialized information that no one else can deliver with equal authority. For example, if you were at a meeting where you were trying to sell a new machine tool, it might be very persuasive to bring along an engineer who had helped develop the tool, even if the engineer wasn't a good communicator. You might not use the poor speaker to deliver most of the information in your presentation, but you might use him or her at certain points—for example, to answer technical questions.

If you plan to have two or more people deliver your presentation, plan in advance who'll deliver each segment. Each person should then mark his or her copy of the presentation to indicate who'll handle each part, so that each of you will be prepared to take over at the right point.

When you come to the end of your segment, you can simply nod to the next speaker, who will then continue. Or each speaker can make a transitional statement to introduce the next speaker:

> John will explain the finer points of this issue.

or,

> Phyllis has been working on the electrical system, and she's the best person to describe its advantages.

HOW LONG SHOULD A PRESENTATION BE?

Lanky Abraham Lincoln said that a man should be tall enough for his feet to reach the ground. We can make a similar comment about the length of a presentation: it should be long enough to tell the audience everything they need—and want—to know.

However, here's a general rule: Keep your oral presentation under twenty minutes. Now, let's explain and refine that generalization.

Most good speakers adhere to the twenty-minute maximum because most audiences begin to get a bit restless after concentrating that long. Naturally, there are exceptions. Some political leaders in some countries can routinely sustain enthusiasm for an hour or two or even more. But for most of us, twenty minutes seems to be about the norm.

There are some situations in which twenty minutes is not long enough; when there is simply too much to cover in so short a time. In those cases, alternatives are available. One alternative is to have one speaker talk for twenty minutes, then turn the presentation over to another speaker. The change of speakers helps the audience relax for a couple of minutes before gearing up for the next bundle of information.

Another alternative is to break for a few minutes. In a small meeting, the speaker might ask for questions, or offer the listeners the chance to get refills on their drinks. In a large meeting, stopping for drinks will take too long, but questions might be in order.

HANDLING QUESTIONS

Taking questions from the audience can be an excellent way of maintaining rapport with them. A question gives the listener a chance to become more deeply involved in your presentation, and therefore to become not just a passive recipient, but an active collaborator.

One decision you'll have to make in advance is whether to invite questions during your presentation. The advantage of taking questions is that it enables you to clarify points your listeners may not understand. (Usually, if one person asks a question about something that's unclear, several people are similarly confused. So, answering these questions may be helpful to the whole audience.)

On the other hand, questions may disrupt the flow of your presentation, and leave many of your listeners confused about your overall organization.

As a general rule, then, in a presentation where you expect the audience to ask questions, it's safest to encourage them to wait until you're done. An introductory comment will usually do the trick:

> I hope you'll write down any questions that occur to you as I go along, and when I'm finished, I'll do my best to answer them in detail.

HUMOR

While it's generally agreed that the judicious use of humor can enliven speeches and oral presentations, I suggest that, as a general rule, it's better to avoid it.

Usually, it's argued that humor relaxes the audience, so that they can pay attention to the important parts of your presentation. On the other hand, if your presentation is well organized, tightly written, and clearly delivered, you will not need to relax them: They will pay attention throughout. And if you are serious during the presentation, your audience will take you seriously. Remember: Being serious does not mean being pompous or being dull. It means communicating worthwhile ideas about worthwhile topics of interest to the audience.

Jokes and anecdotes *can* help to establish rapport with an audience if you tell them *before* the presentation starts. Here are a few suggestions to think about:

- If you tell anecdotes or jokes that poke gentle fun at yourself, and convey a sense of your modesty, the audience will like you the better for it.
- Avoid jokes that cast aspersions on any racial, ethnic, religious or national group, or that refer to stereotypes.
- If possible, use humor that refers to the subject at hand—if you're giving a marketing presentation, use a marketing joke; if you're talking about electronics, use an electronics joke.
- If you can make it believable, phrase the joke as if it were something that actually happened to you: The appearance of reality adds force to virtually any story.
- If you don't know any appropriate jokes, look in the humor section of your bookstore or library, where you will find a variety of humor anthologies.

8. Preparing the Meeting Environment

If you're responsible for setting up the room in which you're going to make a presentation, you can do a number of things to make the audience more receptive. In this chapter, we'll discuss what they are.

INVITATIONS

Even before the meeting begins, you can help to create a favorable impression through the invitations. For example, here's a typical invitation to a routine business meeting:

> From: Bill Hartley
> To: All Task Force Members
> Subject: Monthly Meeting

> The regular monthly meeting will be held on Tuesday, January 14, at 3:00 P.M. in Room 221. Please be prompt.

It's a clear, complete message. The recipients will mark it on their calendars, and dutifully attend at the appointed time. But suppose the message also made them feel that the meeting was going to be unusual, even exciting. Suppose, for example, the memo said:

> The regular monthly meeting is going to feature something really different this time: the new draft of the handbook will be ready to look at—and I think you'll be very happy with it.

> The meeting will be Tuesday, January 14, at 3:00 P.M. in Room 221. I look forward to seeing you then.

The principle is especially valid for invitations to meetings which are not held frequently, such as sales meetings, management conferences and professional seminars. The key to making it a good invitation is the writer's enthusiasm. Enthusiasm makes the recipients feel that they're going, not simply to one more routine gathering, but to an out-of-the ordinary event. And this is a good basic principle to follow in the invitations you write for any meeting: Be enthusiastic.

In a larger organization, one way to transform a routine announcement is with a warm, apparently personal letter (easily managed with the help of a computerized list) from a senior executive, perhaps the president, or the head of a department:

Dear Jim:

It's time to celebrate the terrific work that you and your colleagues have been doing this past year.

I'm very happy to extend this personal invitation to our next annual sales meeting, on February 15, at the elegant Essex House in New York.

We'll be unveiling a dramatic new product that will help keep us—and you—number one in the eyes of your customers. We'll also have some very useful seminars on new sales techniques. And we'll be recognizing and making awards to the top salespeople.

Equally important, this will be a great opportunity for you to meet your friends from the company.

You'll be getting the details from your sales manager soon, but I wanted to send you this personal note to let you know that I'm looking forward to seeing you there.

Best wishes,

That the invitation comes from a top executive is in itself highly motivating: We always feel better when someone important pays attention to us. Further, the letter spells out some of the reasons why the salesperson will enjoy the meeting. These specifics are a way of helping to dramatize the meeting. In general, a personalized form letter is an inexpensive and effective way to announce a meeting to members of any organization.

Another way to create excitement for a meeting is to send out formal invitations. Here's one that announces the theme of the meeting:

The Senior Management of
MULTITASKING MAGNETICS, INC.
Cordially Invites You to
"Quality for a New Decade"
The Company's Annual Marketing Conference
March 20 to March 25
at the Oberst Conference Center
Yakima, Washington

A formal invitation like this, printed on good quality paper, gives the recipient a feeling for the significance of the event—much more so than an impersonal, routine, photocopied announcement. And the form of the invitation reinforces the theme of "Quality for a New Decade." Of course, the envelope should enclose additional necessary information about the meeting.

It would be possible to devote an entire book to the subject of invitations to meetings. But the central concept is a simple one: Your invitation can help make people enthusiastic about the meeting even before they come. Ask yourself: How can I make my invitations do a better job for me?

PREPARING FOR THE SMALLER MEETING

If it's a relatively small gathering, and you're responsible for arranging the room, here's a list of items to check that will contribute to a comfortable, smoothly running meeting:

- Make sure the room is available for the entire time you'll need it. If you need to make special preparations, say, to set up a slide projector, then be certain the room will be available sufficiently far in advance.
- Check to see that there will be enough chairs for everyone. If you're relying on someone else to take care of such details as chairs and ash trays be sure you know in advance who that person is and how to contact him or her before the meeting. And, for insurance, get the name of that person's assistant.
- If the room has air-conditioning and lighting controls, learn how they operate so that you can manipulate them during the meeting if necessary.
- Consider whether you need a microphone. Usually, they're unnecessary for small groups; in fact, they actually detract from the close rapport you want to establish between the speakers and the audience. If you feel amplification will be necessary, test it out in advance of the meeting, and keep it as low as possible so that the audience can hear more of the speaker's unamplified voice. Incidentally, the sound quality of hotel amplification systems is notoriously unreliable. Professional meeting organizers often rent their own high-fidelity systems from local audio supply houses.
- Think about the refreshments you want to offer—coffee, tea, cold drinks and some decaffeinated and low-calorie beverages. You might also ask a local food shop to send up a plate of pastries. Naturally, you'll need cups and plates: Paper or plastic is adequate, but real china adds a bit of class.
- Get to the meeting far enough in advance of its scheduled time to make sure everything has been set up properly—furniture in place, audio-visual equipment working, old coffee cups and pastry crumbs off the table and out of sight.
- If you plan to provide any materials to your audience, such as notepads, pencils, or outlines of the presentation, make sure you have enough, and put them in place.
- If other people from your team will arrive after the audience comes in, it's a courtesy to mention it to your hosts at the beginning: "Marion and Harry will be coming in a few minutes." Ideally, all your people should be present when the audience arrives.

AUDIOVISUAL EQUIPMENT

Chapter 9 discusses how to use audiovisual aids, but before you use them, the equipment has to be available and operational. So if you plan to use audiovisual support, make sure in advance that everything you need will be on hand and working.

If it's critical that your equipment be functioning properly, it will be worthwhile to have backup equipment on hand. This means having duplicate slide or film projectors or videocassette equipment, and yes! even duplicate slides, films or videocassettes. If it's not critical that the equipment be functioning, then plan for what you'll do if the equipment fails.

Decide in advance who'll be responsible for turning equipment on and off, so that your audiovisual imagery can be shown with no interruption in the presentation.

Place projection screens and video monitors where everyone can see them clearly and hear the sound. And, for an extra professional touch, have your slides or films or videocassettes in place and ready to go, so that when the time comes to show them, all you have to do is press a button.

PREPARING FOR THE LARGER MEETING

For a larger meeting, say, forty or fifty or more, you'll probably want to rely on professional help. If you're renting a room at a hotel or conference center, the management will work with you to cover the details.

You may want to hire a professional producer—an individual or a company specializing in putting on meetings for organizations. This subject is covered in greater detail in chapter 11.

One of the largest meeting producers in the country is a company called Caribiner, headquartered in New York City, with branches in Chicago and London. Their brochure, "How to Produce the Quality Meeting," is an excellent guide to the details involved in producing a large meeting. The check list below, adapted from the brochure, provides a detailed list of the items that a professional producer wants to know about any large meeting room. Regardless of the size of your meeting, you'll find in it many items that it will pay you to look for yourself.

Site

Facility _____

Address_____

_____ Telephone_____

Main Contact and Extension_____

His/Her Assistant and Extension_____

Head Houseman and Extension_____

Electrician and Extension_____

Seating Arrangements

Audience Size _____ Banquet in same room?_____

Theater Style _____ Schoolroom Style_____

Labor

Can competent houseman be hired to set up? _____ Rates?_____

Can house electricians run shows? _____ Rates?_____

Can outside labor run house equipment?_____

Names and phone numbers of two local display houses (yellow pages)

_____

_____

Two local suppliers of scaffold_____

_____

_____

Equipment

How many of the following are available? Platforms_____

heights (multiple legs?) _____ widths _____ lengths _____ construction__

Platform steps: how wide?_____ Platforms: carpeted? color?

_____

Tables: heights, widths, length and construction_____

_____

Ladders: heights _____ Cherrypicker: height _____ Lecterns_____

Facility Lighting

Spotlights: Type and wattage_____

Are meeting room lights dimmable? _____ Are they fluorescent?_____

Where are the meeting room lights controlled?_____

Power Requirements

Can facility supply the following power into the meeting room: 3 phase, 5 wire, #4 wire, 60 amps per leg (3 legs), ground (1), neutral (1), bare ends into breakered distribution box?_____

_____

Freight Services

Dimensions of freight elevator that provides service from loading dock to meeting room:

Door dimensions of elevator: width _____ height_____

Inside dimensions of elevator: width _____ depth _____ height _____

If elevator does not go directly into meeting room, check to see whether there are stairs between the freight elevator and the meeting room and also note *all* dimensions of doors through which equipment will have to pass.

Floor Plans

Please obtain a full set of floor plans, together with any available photographs. The plans must indicate: Plan scale ____ Compass "North" ____ Columns or other obstructions including their diameters and distance from each other and all walls ____ Chandeliers and wall sconces including diameters and the height from floor to bottom of chandeliers (all the same)? ____ Can they be removed before the meeting? ____ How much will it cost? _____

Show all ceiling heights, soffits, beams and construction (ask for a reflected ceiling plan)

Floor covering (wood, concrete, etc.)_____

Decor of meeting room_____

Windows, Windowed Doors, Mirrors

Show locations and sizes of all_____

Do the windows have blackout drapes?_____

Do they provide *absolute* blackout? (Test them)_____

Projection Booth

Size of opening _____ Height from booth to bottom of opening_____

Distance from side walls of meeting room to near side of opening_____

_____

Size of booth _____ Can glass be removed?_____

Dividing Walls

Are they soundproof? ____ Are the panels separate? ____ Widths_____

Show where the wall feeds from, where it stores and does it include doors?_____

Balcony

Balcony locations, protrusion width, inside width, balcony floor to railing height, height from main floor to bottom of balcony and main floor to top of railing:_____

Lights, Banners, Cables, Etc.

Show lighting placements on reflected ceiling plan

Can you crawl in ceiling?_____

Has the facility hung anything from the ceiling before?_____

Stage

Supply specific diagrams and pictures showing: Main floor-to-stage height, proscenium opening, width and height, distance from proscenium line to backstage wall.

Don't book any venue without at least 48 uninterrupted hours
for set up and rehearsals

9. Using Visual Aids in Oral Presentations

It is often said that television and the movies have made audiences far more visually sophisticated than they used to be, so that pictures, diagrams and other visuals which accompany today's spoken presentations must be more professional than ever. However, the fact is that audiences still need exactly what they've needed ever since the first stone-age speaker hurled a pointed stick to show how to spear an enemy: visuals that clarify what the speaker is saying.

In this chapter, we'll discuss whether or not you should use visuals; how to prepare visuals for a spoken presentation; and techniques for showing visuals, such as slides, flip charts, and films.

SHOULD YOU USE VISUALS?

Probably the first question to ask yourself is whether you should use visual support, such as slides, or an easel pad or an overhead projector. The answer is yes and no: Yes, if they will help you; no, if they will distract the audience. This still leaves you with the question: When will visuals help, and when will they distract?

As a general rule, visuals will help when you want the audience to remember specific ideas or facts. But visuals may be a distraction when your fundamental purpose is to move the audience emotionally. The distraction can occur because the audience is dividing its attention between you and the visuals when you want them to focus directly upon you.

Of course, many presentations combine both factual and emotional elements. For example, a presentation designed to raise funds for a refugee organization may use photographs to show the plight of the refugees and charts to show the extent of their need. The visuals are factual, but their purpose is to encourage a favorable emotional response.

So where does that leave us? Ultimately it comes down to a question of personal judgment. A rule of thumb is: Use visual support if you can, unless you can think of a good reason not to.

THE BASIC STEPS

In preparing visuals for a presentation, there is a series of logical steps to follow. First, you write the presentation. Then, you decide on the visuals—the photographs, charts, and drawings you'll use. Next, you prepare the visuals yourself, or have them prepared by someone, such as a commercial artist. After that, you review them to make sure that they're right. Then you rehearse with them and make any additional changes you feel are necessary. Finally, you deliver your presentation and accept congratulations on the vividness and clarity of your work. Now, let's go through those steps in detail.

First, write the presentation

As a general rule, it's a good idea not to think about the visuals until you've written the final draft of your presentation. The reason: the purpose of the visuals is to emphasize or clarify your words, and until you're sure of what your words will be, it is difficult to decide what visuals you'll need. If you try to think about the visuals when you're writing the presentation, your focus on the ideas becomes diluted, and you may find it more difficult to organize your ideas logically.

One exception is when you're building your presentation around a series of visuals—say, a group of existing charts. In this case, your presentation will, in effect, serve as captions for the charts. But there is a danger here: the caption type of presentation often becomes a monotonous statistical review. Usually, a better alternative is to select the major points you want to make in the presentation, and then incorporate the charts at the appropriate points to support them.

How the presentation should look on the page

Let's assume that you've written your script, and now you want to select the visuals. To make it easier to decide where your visuals should go, write or type your presentation on the right half of the page, leaving a wide left margin where you can jot down a description of the visuals you'll want to use. (If you're typing, set your left margin at 25 or 30 and your right margin at 60 or 65.)

Keep your paragraphs short. One sentence per paragraph is ideal; three sentences is the maximum you should allow yourself. This will break your ideas into separate segments and allow you to determine more easily just what needs to be visualized.

Another benefit of this format is that it often reveals redundant ideas that were buried in the longer paragraphs and that should be eliminated.

Now you're ready to indicate where the visuals should go.

PUTTING IN THE VISUALS

In the left margin, write a description of the visual you think will clearly illustrate the adjacent paragraph. If you think no visual belongs there, or if you want the same visual as in the previous paragraph, leave the space blank.

What kinds of visuals should you use? Here are the most common kinds.

Key words: Key words are words or phrases that express the main idea of the paragraph. Here's an example. The right column shows the speaker's words, and the left column shows the key word visuals that will be on the screen while those words are being spoken.

WHY ARE WE HERE?	Why have you come here from your homes and offices all across the country?
THREE OBJECTIVES	The reason we are here is to achieve three major objectives.

Keep the wording of your visuals brief—if possible, no more than two or three words. Otherwise, the audience will start focusing on the words and forgetting about you.

Key word builds: A "build" is a series of visuals, each one having an additional line of type. Indicate a build to the artist who's preparing the slide by writing (*Add*) just before the additional words. Here's an example of a key word build consisting of three paragraphs.

LEARN THE PRODUCT (Add)	First, we're going to learn about our new product line.
COMPETITIVE COMPARISON (Add)	Second, we'll learn why it's better than competitive products.
SELLING TO CUSTOMERS	And third, we'll learn how to sell it to our customers.

If your visuals are prepared in advance, you can call attention to each new key word by putting all the words in the build *except* the new key word in one color of type, and making the key word a contrasting color.

Numbers: When visualizing numbers, simplicity is even more important than it is with words. Words, at least, convey a distinct meaning; but numbers convey only the meaning that your words give them. For this reason, show only the numbers that your words explain. Here's an example of a script and an accompanying visual with too many numbers for an audience to understand easily.

MARKETING BACKGROUND	Let's begin with marketing.
TOTAL SALES: $120,000,000	Industry sales last year were 120 million
EAST COAST $80,000,000	dollars, of which 80 million represented East
CENTRAL STATES $10,000,000	Coast sales, 10 million, Central States, and
WEST COAST $30,000,000	30 million, West Coast.

Number builds: Number builds are like key word builds—use them to keep a closely linked series of numbers before the audience. Here's how the previous crammed-up visual looks when done as a number build:

MARKETING BACKGROUND	Let's begin with marketing background. Industry sales last year . . .
(Add)	
TOTAL SALES $120,000,000	were 120 million dollars, of which . . .
(Add)	
EAST COAST $80,000,000	80 million represented East Coast sales . . .
(Add)	
CENTRAL STATES $10,000,000	10 million, Central states . . .
(Add)	
WEST COAST $30,000,000	and 30 million, West Coast

Charts and graphs: Usually there isn't enough room in the margin to show a chart or graph clearly. So simply write in an identifying note, and put the material where you can find it when you're ready to make the actual visuals—for example, attach it to the page, or put it at the end of the presentation.

The same rules apply to charts and graphs that apply to numbers: because they are not self-explanatory, try to show only those elements you're speaking about. Making a build—adding one element at a time to the previous elements—is a good way to explain complex charts and graphs.

Pictures: Here, we're referring to photos, drawings and diagrams. As with charts and graphs, indicate in the margin what pictures you want to show with a paragraph, and if you have the material, attach it to the page, or at the back of the presentation. If you don't have the material on hand, indicate where it can be obtained, if you know.

Here are some suggestions to make pictures look more professional:

• Use only clear pictures. Fuzzy photos, accidental stains, faded colors—all suggest either a lack of care or an amateurishness which will diminish the emotional impact of your presentation.

• Try for consistency in the major dimension of your visuals: Ideally, all should be horizontal or all should be vertical. When you switch from one to the other, it conveys an impression of amateurishness.

• Clean and check your slides and transparencies before showing them. Fingerprints and broken or off-kilter lettering diminish your effectiveness.

Consider logos: You may not want visual support in some sections of your presentation. What should the audience be looking at during those times? You have several options. They can look at the last visual you showed them; this is all right as long as it isn't irrelevant to your new topic. Unfortunately, it frequently is irrelevant—and as a result, it's confusing.

A better alternative is to turn off the machine if you're using slides or an overhead projector, or to turn to a blank page if you're working with an easel pad. This is quite natural and acceptable with an easel pad. But with slides or transparencies, it can create a jumpy, start-and-stop impression.

To overcome this problem, when you're not showing other visuals, consider showing a logo of your organization. It might be the company's name and trademark, or the name of the group you represent, or a theme around which the presentation is built; e.g., "New Doors to New Profits." This provides continuity and serves as an almost subliminal reminder about some important point you want the audience to remember, such as the name of your organization.

PREPARING VISUALS FOR PRESENTATION

Generally, the more professional your visuals look, the more persuasive your presentation will be. For that reason, it's a good idea to have a commercial artist turn your suggested visuals into presentation material. (See chapter 11 for suggestions on selecting an artist.)

The best way to do this is to sit down with the artist and review each of your visuals. A run-of-the-mill artist will follow your instructions exactly. A creative artist will usually suggest improvements on your ideas.

If your visuals consist of nothing more than simple words, charts and numbers, the artist may deliver finished artwork to you or, taking it a step further, finished slides or transparencies. If you have confidence in the artist, this is the least expensive way to proceed.

But if you want to review the artwork before it takes final form, the artist will prepare storyboards—black-and-white, pen-and-ink sketches of the finished visuals. Each sketch will have a number matching a number the artist will have put on your presentation, so you can see where each sketch goes.

For visuals with letters and numbers, ask the artist to show you samples of the type styles she or he proposes to use. Also, ask to see samples of the colors to be used for the letters and numbers and the background on which they'll be placed. (Artists can also prepare storyboards in color—for a substantially higher price.)

If the artwork is to be turned into slides or transparencies for projection, and you don't have your own facilities for making slides, the artist can handle it for you. Alternatively, you can ask the artist to give you the finished artwork, and have a photographic-services company make the slides or transparencies.

Incidentally, the slides we are referring to here are 35mm slides, the virtually universal size. (Polaroid slides are, of course, also used in presentations. While their quality is excellent, the per-slide cost is higher and they require a different-size projector designed for Polaroid slides.)

Your slides can be mounted in cardboard or plastic frames. Cardboard is less expensive, but plastic is less likely to jam in the projector and increases the chances of a trouble-free presentation.

THE LIGHTBOX REVIEW

After your slides are ready, you may find it useful to have a lightbox review. A lightbox is a box illuminated from within. The light shines through a translucent white glass or plastic front which has rows of horizontal ridges to hold slides up against the vertical translucent surface. In a lightbox review, all your slides are displayed at the same time, allowing you to see any gross errors that need correction.

REVIEWING YOUR VISUALS

Whether you're using slides or overhead projector transparencies or a prewritten easel pad or flip chart, rehearse your presentation so that you know precisely which visuals the audience is looking at while you're speaking.

This is relatively easy to do when you're using an overhead projector or an easel pad. It's a bit trickier with slides because usually you cannot see them while you're facing the audience—they are either beside you or behind you.

Further, when you press the button to change a slide, a short interval occurs before the next slide comes up. So, if you're delivering your presentation from a written script, it's a good idea to rehearse by reading aloud and watching the slides as they appear. Then mark on your script the point where you should push the button to make the slide come up precisely at the word you want. Professionals frequently make the mark with a dot of colored ink, or with an adhesive-backed, colored paper dot that can be peeled off and moved at will.

MAKING THE BEST USE OF VISUAL AIDS

To support your oral presentation, you can take advantage of a variety of visual aids. Each offers certain benefits and drawbacks. Let's consider the most popular types.

Slide projectors

The 35mm slide projector is to the professional speaker what the infantryman is to the professional army. It is the basic, reliable workhorse. It's generally used with a carrousel slide tray—a donut-shaped rack which holds eighty slides. (Stack trays—which hold slides in a stack—are also available. But virtually without exception, professionals use carrousels.) Models come with various options, such as adjustable slide-changing speed, automatic focus, and the ability to accept silent, electronic signals from an audio tape, so that the slides change automatically with a taped message. It's also possible to vary the projector lenses to make them suitable for throwing the image longer distances.

Using two or more slide projectors together can make for a more elegant presentation. When a projector changes slides, there is a brief black gap while the new slide replaces the old. Two projectors can be connected and controlled by a switch that turns them on alternately, so that as the projected slide in one machine vanishes, the next slide in the other projector comes on instantly, with no gap. The speed of change can be altered so that the slides dissolve slowly into one another.

Two slide projectors are the most one person can manually control with ease. Three or more projectors, which can create such special effects as animation, are controlled by an audio tape with silent electronic signals placed on the tape where slide changes are wanted. Making these requires the talents of audio-visual specialists discussed in chapter 11.

16mm projectors

When your presentation calls for motion pictures, sixteen millimeter (16mm) is the standard size you'll probably use. Like slide projectors, 16mm projectors come with different lenses for different size screens. They can easily be rented from photographic equipment suppliers.

Filmstrip projectors

Filmstrip is, as its name implies, a strip of film containing individual pictures. Filmstrips can be advanced manually or automatically in step with a recorded audio tape. If you drop a stack of slides, you may have trouble putting them back in correct order; a problem that doesn't exist with filmstrip, and which constitutes one of its advantages over slides. One of its disadvantages is that you can't change the images on a filmstrip, which you can easily do with slides. Also, the images on slides are larger and often clearer.

Videotape

Videotape is becoming a popular means of visualizing presentations. Some speakers use it as a replacement for slides because it permits almost unlimited animation. Thus, where a slide might simply show the number "1" against a contrasting background, a video image could have the number appear to fly in from an infinite distance and vibrate in changing colors against a glowing background. These special effects are not inexpensive, and they require the services of someone skilled in video design and production (see chapter 11).

Video projectors, unlike slide and filmstrip projectors, are quite complex and expensive. Consequently, video images are usually shown on TV sets, or their high-quality versions, monitors.

Portable viewers

You can rent or buy portable machines which project slides, filmstrips or videotapes on their own, self-contained screens. They are generally the size of a large attache case, the screen concealing the projection equipment behind it. Models are available which allow you to advance the visuals manually or automatically. They are generally used for presentations that will be given repeatedly to small audiences—say fewer than ten people—who can be reasonably close to the screen.

Overhead projectors

An overhead projector has a horizontal platform on which you can place a visual that will then be projected to a vertical screen. The visual can be opaque—a magazine page, for example. Or it can be transparent, as with an 8½" × 11" slide. Or you can create your visual on the spot by laying a piece of transparent plastic on the platform and writing on it, with colored pens if you wish. Most overhead projectors are used in conference rooms and classrooms. They are quite useful for showing different kinds of visual materials—some opaque, some transparent, and some to be created on the spot.

Flip charts

Flip charts are, as their name suggests, individual cards or pages designed to be flipped over one at a time, each card revealing new information to the audience. For smaller audiences, they are a highly effective method of supporting the speaker—if the speaker knows how to use them with ease.

Different types of flip charts are suitable for different types of presentations.

Audience of 1–4 people: For the smallest audiences, there are a variety of flip charts which are, in effect, loose-leaf binders with hard covers. The rear cover hinges back to form a firm, vertical support for the pages. The pages themselves are often transparent plastic envelopes which hold and protect the visuals. These are available in office supply and art supply stores.

Audiences of five or more: For larger audiences, you may use an easel pad large enough for everyone to see it clearly. With an easel pad, each page can easily be folded back out of sight as you're finished with it.

Alternatively, you can use individual cards on an easel. As you finish with each card, put it in back of the remaining cards, or lay it down in an inconspicuous spot.

If you're going to make your presentation at a desk or a conference table, an alternative is to use a hinged case to hold the cards. The lid of the case should hinge back and make an acute angle with the base, to which it is then connected by means of a ribbon or strap, forming an inverted V-shaped support for the cards. The cards face the audience, and as the speaker removes each one, he lifts and lays it against the back lid. (See illustration.)

The back surface is facing away from the audience, which cannot see it. So, if on the back of each card are written the words that are appropriate for the card facing the audience, the presenter can simply read them off, dispensing with any other notes.

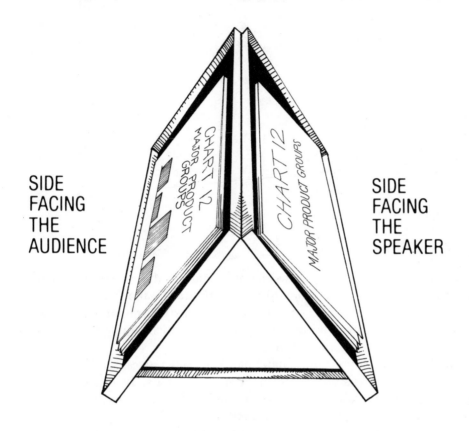

SIDE
FACING
THE
AUDIENCE

SIDE
FACING
THE
SPEAKER

As you finish with a card, you remove it from the side facing the audience and lay it face down on your side, so that the card's back faces you. The notes on the back refer to the new card now facing the audience.

10. Organizing the Meeting

SEVEN QUESTIONS TO ASK

Up to this point, we've been discussing presentations that one or two people can deliver in a relatively short time, from ten minutes to about an hour.

This chapter will discuss a more complex type of presentation, namely, a meeting which contains talks by several people, and which might last anywhere from an hour or two up to several days.

Gatherings of this type go by many names—conferences, seminars, roundtables, discussion groups. They also have many formats. In this chapter, we'll describe the steps involved in organizing the kinds of meetings that companies and other institutions hold most frequently.

Let's begin by assuming that you're an executive who's been assigned to organize a meeting for your company's sales force. There are several questions which you should answer at the very beginning.

1. What is the purpose of the meeting? Every meeting should have one major purpose, just as every sentence should convey one main idea. Summarize this purpose in one or two sentences, and write it down where you can refer to it easily. If the meeting has other purposes, write them down, too. This statement of purpose will help guide you as the meeting develops; in times of confusion, it will remind you of what you're trying to achieve.

Let's say that the main purpose of the meeting is to tell the sales force about a new product your company is introducing. But as you think about it, you realize that you also want to motivate the salespeople to get out and sell the product enthusiastically. You might write down:

> Main purpose of the meeting: To introduce our new product to the sales force. Additional purpose: To inspire enthusiasm for it.

2. Who is the audience? The answer will usually be pretty obvious, but it will be useful to write it down nevertheless. There may be a need to explain it to someone who's not familiar with your audience, and it will be helpful to have it in writing.

You might write down:

Audience: Our whole sales force.

3. How many in the audience? The answer to this question will help you decide how large a room you'll need for the meeting. Audience size will also influence other decisions, for example, the size of the screen you'll need to project visuals that everyone can see clearly. It may also affect the format of the meeting. In a small meeting, for example, it's relatively easy to have a question-and-answer period; in a large meeting it can be much more difficult.

Ask yourself who, in addition to the main audience, should be invited? Also, consider whether the invitees will be encouraged to bring spouses or friends. (Incidentally, if they do attend, the invitations should be phrased that way: "You are invited to bring your spouse or a guest," not "You are invited to bring your spouse.")

4. What seating arrangements? There are two fundamental seating arrangements: theater style, where the audience sits in rows; and schoolroom style, where the audience sits at tables. Schoolroom-style seating requires about one third more more space than theater style, so you'll have to take this into account if you're responsible for obtaining the meeting room.

5. Where will the meeting be held? Here, you'll write down the precise location. This means the state, the city, and address of the building where the meeting will be held, the name of the hotel or conference center, and the names or numbers of the rooms you'll be occupying. If you don't know this information when you start working on the meeting, you'll obviously have to know it before you send out the invitations.

6. When will the meeting be held? Write down the day the meeting will start and the day it will end. Also, if you know it, write down the time it will begin and end on each day.

7. What special equipment will be needed? List the items you know about immediately; for example, a lectern, a microphone, a table, a pitcher of water and tumblers, a slide projector, a movie projector, an easel pad, notepads and pencils for the audience. You'll be asking the people who are speaking at the meeting about their requirements, and you'll add their needs to this list as the meeting develops.

Your answers to the foregoing questions will give you a good start on the meeting. The answers to questions 1 and 2 will help you to focus on its contents. And the answers to questions 3 through 6 will help you determine the kind of space you'll need.

For more information about arranging the physical details of the meeting, read chapter 8, Preparing the Meeting Environment, and pay special attention to the Producer's Site Survey form on pages 72–74. While the form is designed for larger meetings, many of the points it covers can also be helpful for the smaller meeting.

PREPARING AN AGENDA

Meanwhile, you'll also want to put together a meeting agenda—an outline of the sequence of speakers and events. A good way to begin is to list all the speakers and their subjects, if you know them. So, continuing with our assumption that you're responsible for putting on a sales meeting, you might write:

Shirley Johnson, Sales Manager: Sales Goals
Jack Tarburton, Marketing Director: Marketing Background and Competition
Ronnie Ellis, Director of Engineering: Technical Data
Alix Hunter, Advertising Director: Advertising and Promotion Plans
Connie Spritzer, President: Overview: Explanation of What We're Doing

You know there may be other speakers; you also know that some of those you've listed may not be able to make it. But at least you've begun to shape the meeting.

Next, you think about the sequence of speakers. Who should open the meeting; who should close it? Should the others come in any particular sequence?

Looking at the list, you see that the president, Connie Spritzer, should probably come first. Starting with the senior executive is a good idea because it shows the audience that the organization is solidly behind the project. Further, the president's topic—why is the company doing this—is a good subject to begin with, since the people in the audience will want to know why this is a good move for the company to be making.

Jack Tarburton, the marketing manager, looks like a good bet for the second speaker. Jack can give an overview of the market and describe the competition that the new product will be facing.

You decide that the third speaker will be Ronnie Ellis, the director of engineering. Ronnie can explain the new product, and why it's better than anything else on the market.

The fourth speaker, you think, should be Alix Hunter, the advertising and promotion director, who can describe the company's plans to promote the new product.

And the final speaker, Shirley Johnson, the sales manager, will set out the sales quotas, and, as you think about it, should also deliver a rousing conclusion to the meeting.

Now that you have your sequence, you can also assign approximate time lengths for each talk. You know, of course, that not every speaker will abide by them, but it's one more step in putting together a realistic agenda. So, for the moment, you decide that the meeting will begin at 9:00 A.M., and you put together a more detailed agenda. Incidentally, if you date each agenda at the top of the page, you'll avoid confusion later on when you develop newer versions which you may be discussing with others who still have the older versions. Dating the agendas insures that you'll all be talking about the same facts.

On the agenda, leave room to write down any special support the speakers may need—slides, chalkboard, or a demonstration table; anything that will require advance preparation. You'll probably need to discuss this with each speaker before you fill in the column.

Your revised agenda now looks like this:

January 5   AGENDA

Time   *Speaker and Subject*   *Support*

9:00–9:20   Connie Spritzer, President
                          Welcome; Why we're doing this
9:20–9:40   Jack Tarburton, Marketing Manager
                          Marketing Overview; the Competition
9:40–10:00   Ronnie Ellis, Engineering Director
                          Engineering Explanation
10:00–10:20   Alix Hunter, Ad and Sales Promotion Director
                          Advertising and Promotion Campaign
10:20–10:40   Shirley Johnson, Sales Manager
                          Goals and Motivational Wind-up

With your major speakers lined up, you'll want to think about who will introduce them. If each speaker will introduce the next one, your agenda need not be changed. But if you want a master of ceremonies to introduce each speaker, you'll need to add a minute or two between each speaker for the emcee's remarks.

You'll also want to consider whether to have a refreshment break. It's a good idea to schedule one after the first hour or two of the meeting. The agenda above shows that the meeting will be just an hour and forty minutes long. You might have a break after the third speaker, or you might run the meeting straight through without a break. The choice depends mostly on whether you think a break will be helpful, but other factors to consider are the schedule for the rest of the day and the quality of the speakers. If it's a busy day, you may not want to spend the time on a coffee break or if you have a couple of poor speakers, you may want a break in order to give the audience a respite.

Remember to schedule the break long enough for everyone to stand, get refreshments and consume them or go to the bathroom, and return to his or her seat. Generally, this takes about twenty minutes. For a larger meeting, schedule a thirty-minute break, since there will be more milling about.

PREPARING A PRODUCTION SCHEDULE

A production schedule will help you to keep track of the details involved in the meeting. The schedule lists the dates by which each task should be accomplished. A schedule for a simple meeting might look like this. (The numbers before each line are only to make it easier to refer to the commentary which follows.)

Production Schedule

(1) Reserve hotel conference room and guest rooms: October 6
(2) Prepare invitations: November 7–14
       Send invitations: November 15
(3) Memo to speakers: November 15

(4) Speeches or outlines due: December 15
(5) Slide production: December 15–January 1
(6) Lightbox review: January 3
(7) Rehearsal: January 5
(8) Meeting: January 6

Commentary on the production schedule

(1) The larger your meeting, the further in advance you may have to make your reservations. This production schedule calls for making the reservation three months in advance of the meeting. If you're going to need extra time to prepare the conference room for the meeting because, for example, you expect to rehearse there the day before, remember to reserve that time, as well.

(2) The schedule allots about a week for preparing the invitations, and calls for sending them about six weeks before the meeting. Obviously, different meetings will require different times for each of these activities.

(3) If you're responsible for putting on a successful meeting, you may want to be sure that all the speakers have their comments ready in time. Knowing in advance what they're going to say will also give you an idea about whether you should adjust the agenda of the meeting. For example, if someone's presentation is considerably longer or shorter than you'd planned, it may require shifting the coffee break, or possibly even shifting speakers.

Further, if you're responsible for preparing slides or other visuals for the speakers, you'll need time to get it done.

The memo you send to the speakers might read like this:

> Since you'll be making a presentation at the ABC meeting on (date), there are a few things you should know that will help make your talk a success.
>
> Deadlines: Please let me have a copy of your speech or a detailed outline by (date). If you can't make that deadline, please let me know in advance, and we'll work out another deadline.
>
> Visuals: If you plan to provide your own visual support—that is, slides, overhead transparencies, or flip charts—please let me know, so that we can be sure to have the proper equipment on hand.
>
> Rehearsal: Please note that everyone will be present for a rehearsal on (date), which will start at —— o'clock, and finish about —— o'clock. The rehearsal will help to insure that your presentation is smooth and professional.
>
> My staff can help prepare your visuals if you tell us what you need by the deadline date.
>
> A preliminary agenda is attached so that you can see how the meeting is currently planned.
>
> Please call me if you have any questions.

(4) As the speeches or outlines come in, file them in a loose-leaf folder in the sequence in which they'll be presented. This folder is known as a show book, because it contains the details of your show.

(5) If you're responsible for preparing slides or other visuals, give yourself

ample time to have them designed and produced. (Page 79 discusses their preparation in more detail.)

(6) In a lightbox review, you put each speaker's slides on a lightbox, where they can all be seen at once, and any last-minute changes made before the rehearsals begin.

(7) If you can arrange to have a rehearsal, it will usually help the meeting come off more successfully, with fewer embarrassing errors and oversights.

Ideally, the rehearsal should be in the same room as the meeting, and should duplicate the lighting conditions that will be in effect during the meeting. A rehearsal familiarizes the speakers with such details as where to sit before they talk, what path to take to the lectern, and how to adjust the microphone and lights. A rehearsal will also give them a chance to run through their visuals, and make sure that everything's in order.

(8) If you've prepared everything properly, you've gone about as far as you can to insure the success of your meeting. Now you can trust to luck to carry you the rest of the way, for, as the old adage puts it: Luck favors the prepared.

11. Getting Professional Help for Your Presentation

A variety of specialists can help you prepare and deliver a more professional presentation. In this chapter we'll describe what they do, and offer suggestions about how to negotiate prices and deal with them effectively.

WHAT KINDS OF SPECIALISTS ARE AVAILABLE?

Four kinds of specialists are likely to be able to offer the most help: commercial artists, writers, audio and visual suppliers and audiovisual producers.

WORKING WITH ARTISTS

If you're concerned with the appearance of your presentation—the way it will look to your audience—then you may want to call in an artist for help.

If you don't know any artists, you can usually find them in the business yellow pages of the telephone directory, under such headings as Artists, Audio-Visual Production Services, Designers, and Graphic Designers.

Artists can help in many ways. They can provide illustrations for your presentation—and this means everything from charts and graphs to original drawings and paintings. They can also provide you with visuals that may already exist in their own files or in libraries.

In addition, if you'll be distributing printed copies of your presentation, or any other material related to the presentation, they can help to make it look good. For example, they may recommend a special typeface, or suggest a certain kind of paper, or an effective way to bind it.

And if you're delivering an oral presentation, the artist can design the artwork for your visuals; most artists will also take responsibility for delivering the visuals in their final form as slides or transparencies.

How do you find a reliable artist? First, ask acquaintances for recommendations. If that doesn't provide you with names, call some listed in the yellow pages and describe the general nature of your presentation and the kind of help you think you need. (If you're calling a design studio named after an individual, ask to speak to that person.)

When interviewing artists, ask to see samples of their work—preferably, samples of jobs similar to yours. Also, ask for the names of two or three references who have commissioned work similar to yours. And, of course, check those references, and ask whether the quality of the work was satisfactory; the artist met all deadlines; there was any problem with charges; and the firm—and the artist—were intelligent and pleasant to work with.

It's always a good idea to get bids from three artists. And if there is one you like a bit more more than the others, but whose price is too high, consider negotiating.

Artists charge in different ways. They may ask a flat fee for the entire job; or they may charge on a per-piece basis (a certain amount for each piece of artwork) or on a time basis (so much per hour). Generally, the best way to protect yourself is to describe the job fully, then ask for a flat price. Find out what additional costs you might incur if the job should require additional work. If you can't tell the artist at the beginning how much work will be involved, then he or she may prefer to charge on a per-piece or hourly basis.

A few general principles to observe:

• Information is the lifeblood of the professional. Give the artist as much information as you can before you select one, and while you're working with him or her. In fact, one way to judge the quality of a consultant is by the extent and thoroughness of his or her questions. As a general rule, the more questions artists ask, the more information they'll have on which to base their recommendations.

• Unless you know the professional well and have worked with him or her, draw up a formal, written contract, or at least a letter of agreement, signed by both you and the professional, which describes: the nature of the work to be performed; the production schedule—when the job will start, important intermediate dates when major parts of the job should be completed, and the completion date; the payment schedule. One common payment method is one-third when the job starts, one-third when it's half done, and one-third when it's satisfactorily completed. For smaller jobs, payment may be requested only after the work is done. And for longer jobs, the billing may be sent monthly.

WORKING WITH WRITERS

A few professional writers are versatile enough to handle virtually any kind of writing assignment. But most tend to specialize, either in a particular subject or in a particular medium, such as films or articles.

So, if you decide to retain a writer to help with your presentation, be certain that the person has experience in the kind of work you want done. For example, someone who writes excellent magazine articles on a certain industry may be incompetent to write a decent film script on the same subject.

Always ask to see samples of the work of a writer, ideally, work similar to the kind of presentation you're preparing. If you judge that the writer is highly professional, and has an excellent writing style, you probably need be less concerned if he or she has no experience in your field: A good writer can apply his or her skills to virtually any topic.

You can use a professional writer merely to polish a presentation you've already written, or to prepare all of it. If you're asking the writer to polish the presentation, your material should be typed and double-spaced, with wide margins, so that the writer can make the changes easily.

If you're asking the writer to prepare all of it, then be prepared to spend some time explaining what you want included. If you can provide it all from your notes and from your head, expect to spend at least half an hour and perhaps several hours in explanation.

If you're asking the writer to incorporate material that's already in written form, say, in a report or a brochure, indicate specifically what parts of the material you want included. A writer can often do a better job if he or she has background information on the topic, so provide it if you can, through such sources as articles, brochures, books, films, videotape, or previous presentations.

In negotiating a fee with a writer, the best way to protect yourself is to arrange for a flat fee which will cover an original draft and two rewrites. You should figure on two rewrites because the original draft may be all wrong, and the writer may need to start over again, so that the second draft will become virtually another first draft.

A common payment schedule is one-third upon signing a letter of agreement; one-third upon submission of a first draft; and one-third after submission of the final draft. Another common schedule is to pay one-half upon beginning the job, or after submission of the first draft; and the balance after submission of the final draft. For an assignment that is to last for several weeks or months, the writer may prefer to bill monthly.

AUDIOVISUAL SERVICES AND EQUIPMENT

A variety of audiovisual technical specialists can provide different kinds of services and equipment for your presentation. Whatever their specialty, their pricing is usually fixed. Most of them work from simple price charts: You tell them what you need, and they tell you what it will cost.

Audiovisual equipment: Your presentation may require audiovisual equipment, such as slide or movie projectors, overhead projectors or videocassette players and monitors. Or you may be interested in a loudspeaker system. You can rent this equipment from dealers listed in the business yellow pages under such headings as Audiovisual Eqiupment Dealers and Sound Systems and Equipment.

Sound recording services: You may want to include tape recordings in your presentation—for example, a medical presentation might involve doctors' voices; a sales presentation might incorporate customers' comments. Speak to people listed in the yellow pages under Recording Services and Sound Systems and Equipment. Many of them are in fairly specialized fields, and they may not be able to help you, but generally, they can recommend others who can provide what you need.

Film and video services: If your presentation will require films or videotapes, you'll find an abundance of firms that can make them for you. They range from relatively inexperienced beginners who happen to own a video camera, to large organizations with their own staffs, studios and production facilities.

You can find them in the business yellow pages under such headings as Audiovisual Production Services and Video Production Services.

Judging their pricing is generally a simple matter. You describe what you want photographed, and they will give you a price based on the complexity of the job. For example, a single outdoor scene is usually less expensive to shoot than an indoor scene because special lighting is not required. A scene that requires the use of two or three cameras will be more expensive than one that requires only a single camera.

One way of judging the quality of the work is to look at the filmmaker's show reel—a reel of excerpts of previous assignments. When looking at the reel, consider also how effectively it's been put together. Do the sample scenes run on too long, or do they go by so quickly you can't judge them? Both flaws indicate poor film sense. If the filmmaker apologizes for several of the excerpts, it usually signifies lack of experience or lack of ability to control the quality of the work. In either case, be cautious.

Because there are so many film and video producers around, you should plan on interviewing and getting bids from at least two or three before making your choice.

The choice of whether to use film or videotape ought to be made case by case. For example, while film is more expensive, it's generally agreed that it will give a better quality image. This can be important if you're going to present it to a large group, for the film image will be sharper. To a smaller group, the difference may be barely apparent.

This is a matter to discuss with the people you talk to. You may be able to get a more unbiased view from a person who started out in film, since virtually all of these people now use both film and video. Many of those who started out as video producers have had little experience with film, and tend to know little about it.

AUDIOVISUAL PRODUCERS

An audiovisual producer brings together all of the above-listed services—and others, as well—and organizes them on behalf of a client's project. The project may be a simple presentation or it may be a million-dollar extravaganza; it may be designed for an audience of half a dozen people, or for audiences of hundreds of thousands.

Producers generally start out as specialists in one area, such as art, photography, or stage managing, or simply as very good salespeople, and become producers after they get enough experience to understand how a whole project is assembled.

A good producer will begin by developing a firm budget for your project and, if it's necessary, a production schedule so that all the work will be done in time.

Then, the producer will provide whatever help you need to make your project a success—writers, artists, designers, photographers, stage designers, and so on. Where it's appropriate, the producer will also set up and run everything at the presentation site—screens, slide and film projectors, special staging.

Selecting a good producer is not easy. For example, there are advantages to going with small producing companies: Each client is likely to be more important to them because they *are* small. So you will probably get more attention from the top people. On the other hand, a large producer offers you plenty of backup in case any member of the team becomes unavailable.

As a general rule, the size of the producer will not affect the quality of the work. What's more likely to affect it are the qualities of the person who's directly responsible for overseeing your project. If that person is knowledgeable, resourceful and reliable and has a reasonably congenial personality, the work should go well.

How do you make sure you have such a person? You use the same procedures as you do with any other consultant. Talk to several of them. Ask for references. Look at samples of their past projects, especially those similar to your project. And, of course, ask for bids. Incidentally, it's wise not to make your decision solely on the basis of price. If one producer seems much better to you than another, and comes in at a higher price, it may be that you will be getting higher quality work. In this profession as in every other, it is the quality of the individuals who determine the work.